في ذكرى

مارك لينز

Interfaith Series

Series Editor
Joshua Ralston

الإِسْلامُ والنَّصْرَانِيَّةُ مَعَ العِلْمِ والمَدَنِيَةِ

تَأْلِيفُ الأستاذ الإمام الشيخ
مُحَمَّد عَبْدُه (قدَّسَ اللهُ روحَه)
تُوُفِّيَ سنة 1323هـ/1905م

Science and Civilisation Between Islam and Christianity

Muhammad ʿAbduh

Translation and Introduction by
Mohammed Gamal Abdelnour and Umran Khan

GINGKO

First published in English in 2025 by
GINGKO
4 Molasses Row
London SW11 3UX

First published in 1902 in Cairo by Maṭbaʿat Al-Manār under the title
الإسلام والنصرانية مع العلم والمدنية

A CIP catalogue record for this book is available from the British Library.

Hardback: ISBN 978-1-914983-24-5
ebook: ISBN 978-1-914983-25-2

Typeset in Times by MacGuru Ltd

Printed in the United Kingdom by Clays Ltd, Elcograf S.p.A.

www.gingko.org.uk

FSC www.fsc.org
MIX
Paper | Supporting responsible forestry
FSC® C018072

Contents

Foreword

The following work is a translation of the book entitled: *Islam and Christianity with Science and Civilisation* by Muhammad 'Abduh, the most eminent Muslim Arab scholar and reformer in the modern period. His book is a response to claims about Islam made by the former French foreign minister Gabriel Hanotaux and a Lebanese Christian journalist Farah Antun. It has been translated here in full for the first time by Mohammed Gamal Abdelnour and Umran Khan, with notes and a very useful introduction on Muhammad 'Abduh himself and the selected book. In their discussion of 'Abduh's life and works, the translators have relied on the most authoritative sources, most notably *The Complete Works of Muhammad 'Abduh* by Muhammad 'Imārah, one of Egypt's leading present-day scholars.

It is surprising that this important work of 'Abduh has not previously been translated into English, with only some of the views it contains being discussed by interested scholars. As such, the translators of the current volume have filled an important void. Their command of Arabic and English and their knowledge both of the subjects discussed by Muhammad 'Abduh, and of interfaith relations, have allowed them to provide a valuable and elegant rendering of the text. Their assessment of the real views of 'Abduh, as expressed in the introduction, is original, accurate, and noteworthy.

This is a most welcome contribution to knowledge of Islam and Christianity and the debates that arose at the end of the nineteenth and the beginning of the twentieth centuries. The discussion is still relevant to modern interfaith relations between Islam and Christianity. The work will undoubtedly be essential reading for anyone dealing with the subject. I am happy to recommend it to both scholars and general readers alike.

Muhammad Abdel Haleem
Professor of Islamic Studies, SOAS, University of London

Preface

In the last decades of the nineteenth century, it was generally thought in the West that Islam was in serious disarray. In the opening decades of the twentieth century, it was widely accepted that the Muslim world order was in terminal decline. Not only was the Ottoman Empire regarded as no longer sustainable politically or economically, but the religious tradition of Islam was believed to contain inbuilt flaws that made it unsuited to new scientific progress and rational ways of thinking. Missionary organisations typically held the view that the Muslim world was in such a powerless state that, with some common effort, they might achieve the end of Islam for good. In European and American scholarly circles it was commonly agreed that the combining of legal teachings with doctrinal teachings in the Qurʾān rendered them impervious to change and resistant to any development in social and moral thinking. It was to authors who wrote with these assumptions in mind that Muḥammad ʿAbduh replied in the journal articles that were gathered together in this book entitled *al-Islām wa-l-Naṣrāniyya maʿa l-ʿIlm wa-l-Madaniyya*.

The work is one of the most spirited and best informed responses to Christianity written by a Muslim throughout the whole history of encounters. In his arguments, ʿAbduh not only replies fully to the points his opponents make but takes the fight to them by repeatedly showing that if Christianity and Islam are compared, which is what his interlocutors tend to do, his own faith not only matches the other but very often exceeds it. This is apologetics of the most incisive kind. ʿAbduh exhibits his intimate knowledge of the contemporary Christian world by adducing examples that are as least as apt as those he refutes and he shows a command of the history of his own faith and its civilisation that proves unchallengeable.

He sets the unworldliness of Christianity against the rationality and social adroitness of Islam, accepting no criticisms from a religious tradition that he evidently thinks second best to his own. Where he is compelled to admit shortcomings in one or other of the varied forms that Islam has been cast in through history, he has no compunction in attributing this to unwarranted and heretical distortion that often results from alien forces.

Even though he is writing for a journal readership and cannot enter into detailed deliberations, ʿAbduh establishes the basics of a methodology for forward-looking Muslims. Throughout the work, he makes appeals for reference back to the Qurʾān and the models set by the first generations of Muslims. This is only to be expected, but his appeals are to a text that he presents as open and accepting of discussion and to communities of believers that not only tolerated difference but appeared to have regarded it as a necessary part of the religion they followed. Here, he makes a call to fellow Muslims that continues to be relevant. It is this energetic character that gives *al-Islām wa-l-Naṣrāniyya* continuing importance.

David Thomas
Emeritus Professor of Interreligious Relations,
University of Birmingham

Acknowledgements

My relationship with *Imām* Muhammad ʿAbduh (d. 1905) goes back to the fifteen years of my life, from 1997, that I spent at al-Azhar, Cairo, studying Islamic studies and philosophy. Unlike many Azharīs, scholars and students alike, I gravitated intellectually and spiritually towards ʿAbduh's thought. His thought attracted me for three principal reasons. First, the importance he accorded to criticality as well as spirituality concurrently. Secondly, the sense of ‘balance’ embodied in his thought between the past and the present, the *turāth* and the *hadāthah*. Thirdly, my engagement with my mentor and teacher Allāmah Sh Ḥassan al-Shāfʿī (b. 1930), who was my window into ʿAbduh's world; a master who saw himself a student at ‘Abduh's school. Henceforth, I became a friend of ʿAbduh and a guest at his intellectual table for more than fifteen years. Except for al-Abū Ḥāmid al-Ghazālī (d. 1111), not a single Muslim scholar has occupied my mind more than ʿAbduh.

Teaching Qurʾān and *Ḥadīth* Studies at SOAS University of London for four years (2017–2021), ʿAbduh's methodology has always been an integral part of the curriculum I designed. There, inter alia, I would assign an Arabic text by ʿAbduh, translate, and analyse it with the students. Five years ago, among the students taking those courses was my co-translator, Umran Khan. I have a vivid memory of Umran being fascinated by one of ‘Abduh's texts, but equally disturbed by ‘Abduh's misportrayal in Western scholarship, amongst Muslims and non-Muslims alike: ʿAbduh was often portrayed as the ‘Westernised’, ‘modernised’, and anti-*turāth* one.

Aiming to raise the level of the conversation and to disambiguate some of those misconceptions around ʿAbduh, I endeavoured to translate one of his most important Arabic works, which is the text at hand. Discussing this with Umran, he was more than enthusiastic to collaborate with me in this translation. We worked on it for roughly two years. Hence, Umran is the first person in my acknowledgements list. His command of his first language, English, coupled with his deep understanding of Arabic as well as his great sense of commitment, all made our collaborative work an enjoyable trip to ʿAbduh's realm.

I am thankful to Professor Muhammad Abdel Haleem who encouraged us to go ahead with the project and was astonished that the text had not already found its way into English scholarship. Not only that, but he kindly wrote a generous Foreword to the translation. Similarly, Professor David Thomas who shared the same excitement as Abdel Haleem, rigorously wrote a Preface to the translation.

We are deeply grateful to our publisher, Gingko, represented by Dr Barbara Schwepcke and Mr Harry Hall, for believing in the manuscript and for accepting it as part of their Religion Series, edited by Dr Joshua Ralston. Also, we were particularly lucky to have had Dr Stephen Landrigan, the author of *Shakespeare in Kabul*, to have been our copy-editor. Gratitude goes also to Nadja Harvard, who facilitated the process at Gingko, and to the anonymous peer reviewers who greatly enhanced the quality of the translation with their reviews and feedback.

Last but not least, I am thankful to my long-term interlocuters who share with me a sense of admiration for ʿAbduh: My beloved wife, Mai Bakr, with whom I have read and discussed several texts of ʿAbduh. My dear friends Dr Muhammad al-Sayyad and Dr Walid Ghali; the former's engagement with ʿAbduh's thought is eye-opening and the latter's deep interest in ʿAbduh's ideas sparked his groundbreaking workshop on ʿAbduh (April 2024) at Agha Khan University, London. My fellows and friends in Bath Mosque with whom I enjoyed multiple conversations about this subject.

I am deeply grateful to Professor Gavin D'Costa and Dr. Toby Matthiesen for their generosity in granting me affiliation to the University of Bristol, which made this project possible. My heartfelt thanks also go to Jacky Colliss Harvey for her meticulous editing and invaluable support in refining this work.

Finally, I would like to end this acknowledgement by stating that ʿAbduh was probably, according to the English poet and writer Wilfrid Blunt (d. 1922), among the first Egyptians to have come to London. So, by translating his Arabic work into English, we will hopefully have contributed to connecting Cairo to London at a time of polarisation and dichotomisation.

والله يقول الحق وهو يهدي السبيل

Dr Mohammed Gamal Abdelnour
Bath Spa, 2024

I first began my serious study of ʿAbduh in Dr Gamal's classes at SOAS, University of London. My interest in ʿAbduh has primarily continued through discussions with Dr Gamal about his own studies of ʿAbduh, along with further readings of 'Abduh's works. As such, I must first acknowledge the debt I owe to Dr Gamal for introducing me to 'Abduh and for reaching out to me to collaborate on this translation. For me, the project was an opportunity to work with two of my most influential teachers, 'Abduh and Dr Gamal.

I share Dr Gamal's gratitude to all those mentioned who enabled this project to come together by contributing forewords, editing the text, or seeing through the process of publication.

Lastly, I am forever indebted to my parents for their support of my Arabic studies, which would not have otherwise been possible. My wife, who dutifully looked after our baby daughter, Aamina, while I would spend the evenings working on the translation. My friend and fellow Arabic student Andrew Knight, with whom I discussed the translation throughout the process.

I share Dr Gamal's sentiments and am hopeful that this translation will play a role in dispelling the misunderstandings around 'Abduh that have become so widespread.

Umran Khan
London, 2024

«(. . .) وهذا الكلام في نهاية الحكمة والبلاغة وكثرة المعاني مع نقله من لغة إلى لغة، فكيف به وهو على لغة قائله!؟»

ابن النديم معلقاً على حِكَم أوردها لأرسطو

"And these [translated] words are at the very peak of wisdom and pinnacle of eloquence; although they are merely translations from one language to another, they remain rich in meanings; how much more so when it is in the language of its author?"

Ibn al-Nadim commenting on a series of wisdoms ascribed to Aristotle. We hope it equally applies to the text at hand.

Translators' Introduction

Muhammad ʿAbduh (d. 1905) is a central figure to modern Islam. Much of modern Muslim thought has been a reaction either for or against his ideas. However, in the last few decades, his ideas have often been presupposed rather than being discussed, which creates ambiguity and confusion as to what he really proposed. Moreover, much of this confusion lies in the fact that out of ʿAbduh's complete oeuvre, only one work has been fully translated from Arabic into English, that is, *Risālat al-tawḥīd* (Theology of Unity). Addressing this gap, the present monograph aims to translate one of his most famous works, namely, *al-Islām wa-l Naṣrāniyya maʿa al-ʿIlm wa-l-Madaniyya* (Science and Civilisation Between Islam and Christianity) – a treatise that has occupied the specialists of ʿAbduh's day and the masses alike.

Before we delve into the translation, an introduction to ʿAbduh's context is apt. This introduction is composed of three parts. First, a biographical section introduces him and places him within a historical and intellectual context. Secondly, an epistemological section deals with the intellectual content of his work that is presented here, arguing that this treatise is one of epistemology, as opposed to the common perception of it as an apologetic treatise. Thirdly, a brief mention is made of our style of translation and the edition we used.

Biographical context

There are six key chapters to ʿAbduh's life.[1] First is his upbringing and formative education. ʿAbduh was schooled in al-Azhar, where he received

1 Muhammad ʿImāra, *al-Aʿmāl al-kāmila li'l-imām Muḥammad ʿAbduh*, 1st edn, Vol. 1, (Cairo and Beirut: Dār al-Shurūq, 1993), pp. 22–3.

a traditional education and earned the title of a *ḥāfiz* (someone who memorises the Qur'ān by heart) at the age of twelve.[2] However, he was disenchanted by the Azharite education in both form and content. He disliked the method of teaching due to its overemphasis on learning by rote without providing enough intellectual engagement with the content. Additionally, the content itself, which comprised mostly of commentaries on old texts, did not appeal to him either. As a result, and against his father's wishes he decided to abandon his studies when he was about sixteen years old.[3]

The second stage of his life is linked to his encounter with Shaykh Darwīsh, a maternal uncle and a local Ṣūfī master, who persuaded him to return to his Azharite education. In later years, ʿAbduh wrote of Darwīsh's impact on him: 'He released me from the prison of ignorance into the free space of knowledge, from the chains of *taqlīd* (the unverified imitation of preceding scholars) to the freedom of [belief in] the Unity [of God] … He was the key to my happiness, if I ever had any happiness in my life. He gave me back that intuitive part of myself which I had lost, and revealed what was concealed to me in my own nature.'[4] Having had that Ṣūfī experience and been redrawn to scholarship, he initially chose to live a life of solitude from everything save his studies, shunning contact with other humans such that he would seek God's forgiveness if he unnecessarily spoke to anyone.[5] However, he was rescued from the danger of this solitude, first by another intervention of Shaykh Darwīsh, and then by his first meeting with Jamāl al-Dīn al-Afghānī (d. 1897).[6] The latter was not only a man of scholarship but primarily a political activist who travelled across the Muslim world during the late nineteenth century, advocating Pan-Islamic unity against forces of colonialism.[7]

2 Ludwig W. Adamec, *Historical Dictionary of Islam,* 3rd edn (London and New York: Rowman, 2017), p. 22.

3 Rashīd Riḍā, *Tārīkh al-imām Muḥammad ʿAbduh*, 2nd edn, Vol. 1, (Cairo: Dār al-Faḍīla, 2006), p. 20. See also: ʿImāra, *al-Aʿmāl al-kāmila*, Vol. 1, pp. 22–3 and Emad Hamdeh, 'Shaykh Google as Ḥāfiẓ al-ʿAṣr The Internet, Traditional "Ulamā", and Self Learning', *The American Journal of Islam and Society*, Vol. 37, No. 1–2 (2020):79.

4 Riḍā, *Tārīkh al-imām*, p. 23.

5 Riḍā, *Tārīkh al-imām*, p. 24.

6 Albert Hourani, *Arabic Thought in the Liberal Age 1798–1939* (London: Oxford University Press, 1962), p. 131.

7 Vali Reza Nasr, *The Sunni Revival: How Conflicts within Islam Will Shape the Future* (New York: Norton, 2006), p. 103.

Encountering al-Afghānī in the late 1860s shaped the third stage in ʿAbduh's life.[8] ʿAbduh greatly admired the vastness of al-Afghānī's knowledge and the philosophical underpinning of his thought. He later became his most devoted student and the main propagator of his ideas. During this time, ʿAbduh also began to be known as a commentator on religious, social, and political subjects in the renowned *al-Ahrām* journal (The Pyramids).[9] In 1877, he graduated from al-Azhar with the degree of *ʿālim* (scholar), to begin his career as a teacher, which was always to be the most likely profession for him.[10] However, he taught not only at al-Azhar, but also held informal classes in his home.[11] Additionally, in 1878 he was appointed as a history lecturer at Dār al-ʿUlūm, which was newly set up to provide a modern education for Azharite students who aspired to become judges or teachers in state schools.[12] The books that he read and taught during this period reflect his evolving mindset, embodying a hybridity in his thought that aimed to reconcile Islamic epistemology with foreign sources of knowledge, whether classical Greek or modern European. Among the books he taught in his house were a work on ethics by Ibn Miskawayh (d. 1030)[13] and the Arabic translation of François Guizot's *History of Civilization in Europe*.[14] On the other hand, at Dār al-ʿUlūm, he taught Ibn Khaldūn (d. 1406)[15] through his *Muqaddima* (The Introduction).[16] Of traditional theological works, he had a favourable view of the *Catechism* written by al-Sanūsī (d. 1490), who was a formidable scholar of Islamic

8 ʿImāra, *al-Aʿmāl al-kāmila*, Vol. 1, pp. 24–5.
9 ʿUthmān Amīn, *Muḥammad ʿAbduh: rāʾid al-fikr al-miṣrī* (Cairo: al-Majlis al-ʿAlā li'l-Thaqāfa, nd), p. 30.
10 Riḍā, *Tārīkh al-imām*, pp. 25–6.
11 Riḍā, *Tārīkh al-imām*, p. 136.
12 Riḍā, *Tārīkh al-imām*, pp. 135–6.
13 Ibn Miskawayh was a philosopher and historian who hailed from Persia. In terms of philosophy, he was a Neoplatonist and his influence on Islamic philosophy is chiefly in the area of ethics. See Oliver Leaman, *The Biographical Encyclopedia of Islamic Philosophy* (London: Bloomsbury, 2015), pp. 323–6.
14 Leaman, *Biographical Encyclopedia*, pp. 103–4. See also: Hourani, *Arabic Thought*, p. 132.
15 Ibn Khaldūn was an Arab philosopher, sociologist, and historian. He is widely recognised as one of the most accomplished social scientists of premodern philosophy, and regarded by many as the father of historiography, sociology, economics, and demography studies. See Leaman, *Biographical Encyclopedia*, pp. 199–204.
16 Leaman, *Biographical Encyclopedia*, p. 136.

theology. ʿAbduh held that it is the duty of the faithful to know the articles of Islamic creed by familiarising oneself with this *Catechism.*[17] Commenting on this selection of books, Albert Hourani wrote: 'The choice of books shows the way in which his mind was moving: Miskawayh's book was an Islamic version of Greek ethical philosophy and both Guizot and Ibn Khaldūn dealt in different ways with the problem of the rise and fall of civilizations.'[18]

The fourth stage in his life is marked by his independence after al-Afghānī was exiled from Egypt and ʿAbduh had to chart out his own programme of reform, to become a shaper of public opinion and a participant in Aḥmad ʿUrābī's (d. 1911) Protest during the 1870s and early 1880s.[19] ʿAbduh's early articles in *al-Ahrām* largely mirrored al-Afghānī's political views. This was perhaps the reason that ʿAbduh was ordered to retire to his village when the Khedive Tawfīq exiled al-Afghānī from Egypt.[20] Nevertheless, in 1880 ʿAbduh was brought back to Cairo to become an editor, then an editor-in-chief, of *al-Waqāiʿ al-miṣriyya* (The Egyptian Affairs) – Egypt's official gazette.[21]

Before moving onto the fifth period in ʿAbduh's life, a word on his participation in ʿUrābī's Protest is needed. Typical of many men of education and scholarship, ʿAbduh was initially against any revolutionary solutions if real political and social reform was the goal. In fact, he attempted many times to convince ʿUrābī not to revolt for two key reasons: his fear of foreign intervention, and his concerns that the masses were not ready yet to participate in the running of the state. He saw the Protest as jeopardising

17 Charles C. Adams, *Islam and Modernism in Egypt: A Study of the Modern Reform Movement Inaugurated by Muḥammad ʿAbduh*, 2nd edn (New York: Russell, 1968), p. 116. This *Catechism* is one of the traditional post-Ghazālian textbooks that are still today taught in al-Azhar. This fact sheds doubt on Khaled el-Rouayheb's assumption that ʿAbduh disregarded 'the entire course of Islamic theology after al-Ghazāli as confused, misconceived, and pedantic', El-Rouayheb, *Islamic Intellectual History in the Seventeenth Century: Scholarly Currents in the Ottoman Empire and the Maghreb* (New York: Cambridge University Press, 2015), p. 202.

18 Hourani, *Arabic Thought,* p. 132.

19 ʿImāra, *al-Aʿmāl al-kāmila*, Vol. 1, pp. 27–8.

20 This is an honorific title associated mostly with the grand viziers of Egypt from 1805 to 1914. See Adam Mestyan, 'Khedive', *Encyclopaedia of Islam*, 3rd edn, Vol. 2 (Leiden: Brill, 2020), pp. 70–71.

21 Hourani, *Arabic Thought,* p. 133.

the internal reform with which he had occupied himself for more than a decade by then.[22] However, when the Protest became a public cause, he did not hesitate to support it.[23] After the Protest was aborted and ʿAbduh's fears became realities, he was not only incarcerated but also maltreated. This, 'and the collapse of the nationalist movement, had a profound effect on him,' such that his 'great intellectual strength [was] overclouded for a time by moral and physical weakness. His mind and body alike seemed crushed out beyond hope of recovery by the cruel reaction born of shipwrecked hopes and the agony of despair.'[24] Despite this, ʿAbduh's reaction to maltreatment and incarceration challenges the perception that assumes a relation between maltreatment and a turn towards violence and extremism.[25]

The fifth stage of ʿAbduh's life heralded his engagement with the outside world, when he was exiled for three years in Beirut and then joined al-Afghānī in Paris.[26] There he helped al-Afghānī organise his intellectual society and publish *al-ʿUrwa al-wuthqā* (The Firmest Bond). He also visited London in 1884 and met with a few philosophers and politicians including Herbert Spencer; he wrote letters to Leo Tolstoy and Isaac Taylor, and read Jean-Jacques Rousseau and Ernest Renan, as he also learned to read French. In Beirut, ʿAbduh gave his lectures on theology, which later formed his magnum opus, that is, *Risālat al-tawḥīd* (Theology of Unity) and co-formed a secret association of ecumenism between the three monotheistic religions: Judaism, Christianity, and Islam.[27]

The sixth and final stage of his life began in 1888 when he was allowed to come back to Egypt.[28] Although he had wished to return to teaching, the Khedive feared his influence over future generations, and hence denied him teaching duties. Instead, he was appointed as a judge in the local courts set up in 1883 to spread the new codes of positive law, marking the beginning of a new public mission which remained until his death in

22 Riḍā, *Tārīkh al-imām*, pp. 144–50.
23 Amīn, *Muḥammad ʿAbduh*, p. 36.
24 Hourani, *Arabic Thought*, pp. 133–4.
25 See for instance, Shahrough Akhavi, 'Sayyid Qutb', in *The Oxford Handbook of Islam and Politics*, eds John L. Esposito and Emad El-Din Shahin (Oxford: Oxford University Press, 2013), pp. 159–69.
26 ʿImāra, *al-Aʿmāl al-kāmila*, Vol. 1, pp. 28–32. See also Amīn, *Muḥammad ʿAbduh*, p. 37.
27 Amīn, *Muḥammad ʿAbduh*, pp. 39–40.
28 ʿImāra, *al-Aʿmāl al-kāmila*, Vol. 1, pp. 32–6.

1905, and during which he had a chance to reform the religious courts and restructure the *awqāf* (religious endowments). His positions on questions of public concern, including religious education and marital relations, were also of relevance during this time. Moreover, he founded and managed the *Muslim Benevolent Society*, which aimed to establish private schools and help the poor and destitute. In 1895, he persuaded the Khedive to set up an administrative council for al-Azhar, where he was its most prominent voice for a decade, implementing reforms in its regulation.[29] He collaborated with one of his closest associates, Rashīd Riḍā (d. 1935) in a Qur'ān commentary based on his lectures in al-Azhar but he only finished up to Qur'ān 4:125. As his death approached, Riḍā completed the commentary singlehandedly.[30]

Intellectual content: apology or epistemology?

ʿAbduh's *al-Islām wa-l Naṣrāniyya maʿa al-ʿIlm wa-l-Madaniyya* (Science and Civilisation between Islam and Christianity) has often been seen as a work of apology. As a genre, the key aim of apologetics is to defend religious doctrines and practices through systematic argumentation and discourse, which has its roots in Christian theology.[31] However, works of Islamic theology (*Kalām*) are also often seen as belonging to that genre as well. Two recent academic studies on ʿAbduh that have examined this treatise view it as one of apology. Ammeke Kateman's *Muḥammad ʿAbduh and His Interlocutors: Conceptualizing Religion in a Globalizing World* (2019) and Oliver Scharbrodt's *Muhammad 'Abduh: Modern Islam and the Culture of Ambiguity* (2022) argue that ʿAbduh, throughout the treatise, not only defends Islam in opposition to Christianity, but also offers some scathing critiques of the Christian tradition.

These conclusions, while understandable, are not the views that we, the translators, endorse. What we propose is that *al-Islām wa-l Naṣrāniyya* is a work of *epistemology*, rather than an *apology*. Three key reasons support

29 Hourani, *Arabic Thought,* pp. 134–5.

30 Muhammad ʿAbduh and Rashīd Riḍā, *Tafsīr al-manār* 2nd edn, Vol. 1, (Cairo: Maṭbaʿat al-Manār, 1947), p. 14.

31 See John M. Frame, *Apologetics to the Glory of God* (Phillipsburg: Presbyterian & Reformed, 1994).

this reading. Firstly, while it is true that ʿAbduh critiques the Christian tradition in this treatise, he also directs some scathing criticisms against the Islamic tradition itself. Therefore, viewing it as merely a work that aims to defend the Islamic tradition does not do justice to ʿAbduh's equal interrogation of his own tradition. Secondly, reading it as a work of apology, rather than epistemology, disconnects it from ʿAbduh's earlier works. In those earlier works, either his Qur'ān commentary or in his *Risālat al-tawḥīd*, he shows a deep appreciation of the Christian tradition and offers a reading that takes Christianity, as it is, as a valid path to truth and salvation, despite being critical of certain aspects of it.[32]

Thirdly, the *islām* that ʿAbduh defends in this epistle differs from the dominant understanding of it. While the common usage of the term refers to Muhammadan Islam, in his interpretation of Q3:85, which reads: 'if anyone seeks a religion other than *islām*, it will not be accepted from him: he will be one of the losers in the Hereafter,' ʿAbduh argues that confusing *islām* here with Islam is not only inaccurate but is also an act of theological prejudice. Salvation is based on the former rather than the latter. That is, living in a state of submission to God, and not merely belonging to the religion that is formally called Islam, is what puts one on the path of salvation. This is what is meant when the Qur'ān depicts Abraham (and other prophets as well) as being Muslim, or ones who submit to God. Therefore, the Qur'ānic view of a 'true' Muslim is one whose faith in God is pure and who does not ascribe any other partners to Him.[33] Hence, one cannot say that ʿAbduh was defending Islam – as commonly understood – against Christianity. More importantly, his redefined *islām*, as opposed to Islam, does not exclude Christianity as such, but rather includes it in God's plans of truth and salvation. Therefore, viewing those dynamics as ones of apologetics does not do justice to ʿAbduh's overall epistemic paradigm.[34]

In *al-Islām wa-l Naṣrāniyya*, ʿAbduh engaged in two debates through

32 See Mohammed G. Abdelnour, *A Comparative History of Catholic and Aš'arī Theologies of Truth and Salvation: Inclusive Minorities, Exclusive Majorities* (Leiden and Boston: Brill, 2021), pp. 140–44.

33 ʿAbduh and Riḍā, *Tafsīr al-manār*, 2nd edn (Cairo: Maṭbaʿat al-Manār, 1947), pp. 360–61.

34 See Abdelnour, *A Comparative History of Catholic and Aš'arī Theologies of Truth and Salvation*, pp. 140–44; Abdelnour, *The Higher Objectives of Islamic Theology: Toward a Theory of Maqāṣid al-ʿAqīda* (Oxford and New York: Oxford University Press, 2022), pp. 77–96.

the medium of the press. One was in response to a number of articles written by the former French foreign minister Gabriel Hanotaux (d. 1944) on Islam's relation to civilisation, as compared with Christianity's. The other came in response to articles by the Lebanese Christian author Farah Antun (d. 1922) on Islam's position on tolerance vis-à-vis Christianity and how this impacts the way both traditions treat scholars and scholarship. In both responses, ʿAbduh analytically and critically interrogates and integrates criticisms put forward by Orientalists and Arabs who were somehow Europeanised, most notably Antun.[35]

Beginning with Hanotaux, Rashīd Riḍā in his *Tārīkh al-Ustādh al-imām al-Shaykh Muḥammad ʿAbduh* (Biography of Muhammad ʿAbduh) tells us that it was one of ʿAbduh's quotidian habits to go through the day's newspapers on the train from Al-Azhar – where he taught in the afternoon – back to his home in ʿAin Shams, in eastern Cairo. It was in April 1900 that ʿAbduh was agitated by Hanotaux's article on Islam, which had been translated into Arabic and published in the Egyptian newspaper *al-Muʾayyad* (The Aided). However, his concern did not get the better of him. Instead, he began writing a response as dinner was being prepared for him and completed it after dinner, then sent it the next morning to *al-Muʾayyad*, which then published it.[36] Kateman tells us that ʿAbduh was not the only intellectual who was agitated by Hanotaux's article about Islam. For weeks, if not months afterwards, this continued to be a leading story in several Egyptian newspapers, most notably *al-Muʾayyad*, *al-Ahrām* (The Pyramids), and *al-Liwāʾ* (The Flag), with writers contributing to the discussion, either in agreement with ʿAbduh or with Hanotaux.[37]

To contextualise this intellectual, intercultural, and interreligious exchange, we may take a step back to note that Hanotaux published two articles in French in *Le Journal* in 1900. Having categorised Islam as a Semitic religion, as compared with Christianity which he argued is an Aryan religion, he contended that Semitic and Aryan peoples have different

35 Oliver Scharbrodt, *Muhammad ʿAbduh: Modern Islam and the Culture of Ambiguity* (London: I.B. Tauris, 2022), pp. 188–9.

36 Rashīd Riḍā, *Tārīkh al-imām Muḥammad ʿAbduh*, 2nd edn, Vol. 2 (Cairo: Dār al-Faḍīla, 2006), p. 400.

37 Ammeke Kateman, *Muḥammad ʿAbduh and His Interlocutors: Conceptualizing Religion in a Globalizing World* (Leiden and Boston: Brill, 2019), p. 163.

conceptions of divinity which naturally led to their respective contemporary realities. That is, Semites highlight divine transcendence which not only assumes an inherent gap between God and Man, but also leaves too much room for a fatalistic resignation before God's will and little room for human intervention in the management of the world. While Islam fell prey to such issues, Christianity overcame its Semitic roots by adopting and adapting an Aryan conception of God that highlights divine immanence in the world and maximises human intervention in running its affairs. This adaptation manifests itself greatly in the Christian belief in Jesus Christ being the incarnate son of God, leading to an optimistic attitude towards life, as opposed to a fatalistic one.[38]

Kateman and Scharbrodt both show how ʿAbduh deconstructed these flimsy correlations. Taking the legitimacy of these categories as given due to them being accepted as scientifically accurate in his era, ʿAbduh argues that both peoples, the Aryans and the Semites, have intermingled throughout history so much so that their differences can barely be identified. In his responses, ʿAbduh resorts to history to say that it does not support Hanotaux's theory in that there have been prosperous and advanced Semites, and the opposite has been true for some Aryans. An example of the former, he states, are the Jews and ancient Phoenicians, in contrast to Indians, who despite being of Aryan origin, are deemed backward by the Europeans.[39] More topically, the Islamic civilisation, in spite of its belief in divine transcendence and divine predestination, produced a great civilisation, and it was upon its foundations that European civilisation was anchored. It did so, not by separating itself from neighbouring civilisations, but rather by integrating the sciences of antiquity, most notably those of the Persians, Egyptians, Romans, and Greeks.[40]

While we are in affinity with much of what Kateman and Sharlbrodt had to say here, we depart from their analysis in viewing ʿAbduh's response

38 Scharbrodt, *Muhammad ʿAbduh,* p. 189.

39 As noted by Michael Witzel, 'The use of the word Ārya or Aryan to designate the speakers of all Indo-European (IE) languages or as the designation of a particular "race" is an aberration of many writers of the late 19th and early 20th centuries and should be avoided.' See Witzel's 'Autochthonous Aryans? The Evidence from Old Indian and Iranian Texts', *Electronic Journal of Vedic Studies* Vol. 7, No. 3 (2001): 3, http://dx.doi.org/10.11588/ejvs.2001.3.830.

40 ʿImāra, *al-Aʿmāl al-kāmila*, Vol. 3, pp. 223–6.

as a form of apologetics. That is to say that ʿAbduh goes far beyond this mere point-by-point response to explain the essence of the two traditions from an epistemic, not an apologetic, perspective. To this end, he not only interrogates Hanotaux's claims, but also takes a critical position of the Islamic tradition itself. That is, he does not deny the current intellectual decay and political corruption which permeate the Muslim world and he notes the Muslims' need for reform. However, this reform does not lie in imitating Europe, as Hanotaux and Antun contend, but rather in going back to the 'golden age' of Islam, with a view to retrieving the real intellectual and cultural values that it inhabited.[41]

In doing so, he takes us beyond the specific theologies of Christianity and Islam and shows that they both were somehow products of history, and that other factors in history itself may impact the making of a tradition, aside from its foundational scriptures. That is, a passivist or an activist attitude towards the universe does not hinge solely upon whether one believes in divine transcendence or divine immanence, but rather on how one makes sense of the extent of divine omnipotence and divine omniscience. Moreover, with divine omnipotence and omniscience, both traditions have developed miscellaneous theological responses, making it almost impossible to speak of uniform or fixed views on those questions. Therefore, Christianity and Islam were prone to the same problems that were faced by other philosophical and theological traditions. To ignore this is to ignore how historical dynamics and contexts influence theological responses. It is worth quoting ʿAbduh verbatim here:

> The issue of predestination is not confined to a single group, anthropomorphists or those who affirm God's transcendence, as those two issues have nothing to do with this matter. Rather, the genesis of this debate in theology is God's omniscience and omnipotence – whether God's knowledge encompasses everything and the extension of His power to all possibilities. The dispute among Christians themselves in this matter was significant, and they are anthropomorphists in Monsieur Hanotaux's view. The debate between them started before Islam and continues until the present day. Perhaps

41 ʿImāra, *al-Aʿmāl al-kāmila*, Vol. 3, p. 250.

Hanotaux could study Thomists – followers of Saint Thomas Aquinas (d. 1274) – or the Dominicans, as they are all determinists, and the Jesuits who are libertarians. Each of these views has representative groups among the Christian denominations and it is not a Semitic issue, as he claims. Rather, its roots sprouted and its branches grew among the Aryans, and then their contagion spread to others.

Have you heard of a Jew lying flat on his back, abandoning all action while relying solely upon predestination? Have you heard of a single Phoenician – whose rowboats had reached the British Isles – who slept and indulged in his dreams depending solely on what the unseen would lead him to? Yet, we have heard of this in monasteries and among the friars, and we know stories of numerous individuals who relied solely on the support of others until Europe reached a point where it raised an outcry against them and demanded their forceful removal.

The school of philosophy among the Greeks that argued for chance and arbitrariness became well-known and is even familiar to novices in philosophy; the refutation of which is the starting point of philosophical literature. It is the view of those who contend that things exist due to chance or non-contingence and that which is possible does not require a reason to exist. Is this not more worthy of belonging to Determinism than attributing all matters to the Creator of the universe? Does this school really elevate its Aryan proponent to attaining a high standing and a place of honour?

The Qur'ān – the revealed scripture of Islam – censures and rebukes determinists. It critiques their statement: 'If God had willed, we would not have ascribed partners to Him – nor would our fathers – or have declared anything forbidden,' by saying: 'in the same way, those before them continually denied [the truth] until they tasted Our punishment. Say, 'Have you any knowledge that you can show us? You follow only supposition and tell only lies.' It affirms the doctrine of man's acquisition of his acts and of free choice in almost sixty-four verses. Anything which it mentions that could cause one to imagine the opposite of that was only mentioned to affirm the general Divine habit, known as the universal laws of nature, as in the verse: 'If God had so willed, He would have made you one community,' and other comparable passages.

> … Alas! The egos of certain Muslim leaders were inflated in a manner akin to prideful devils and they took up the scum from the filth of the Aryans and polluted the pure earth and contaminated its surface; its impurity proliferated and its contemptibility spread extensively.[42]

While Hanotaux contends that for Muslims to advance, they need to follow European societies in separating political from religious authority, ʿAbduh thinks that this is a mere projection of the European Christian experience onto the Muslim world, which has a different historical experience.[43] However, this does not mean that the secular and the religious are completely fused in Islam. What it essentially means is that Islam not only provides spiritual guidance but also political guidance, but this political guidance is there to *guide* and not to *govern* as such. Therefore, we can say that an equivalent of the medieval institution of the papacy in its political power did not exist in the Islamic tradition. As for the institution of the caliphate, ʿAbduh considers the caliph as 'a civil ruler' (*ḥākim madanī*) – his mandate does not extend to creedal matters but solely to matters of the state. As Scharbrodt puts it, 'ʿAbduh's designation of caliphal or sultanic authority as civil denotes neither a secular reading of Islamic modes of governance, as suggested by Haddad, nor the primacy and comprehensive nature of Islamic law, as argued by Rida.'[44] In this, his view is more akin to pre-modern Islamic political philosophy, where the ruler needs to enforce Islamic law, but does not possess any authority over matters of faith. Therefore, invoking the European model of separation is irrelevant to the Muslim context, for the two realms, the secular and the religious, were not initially combined.[45]

Farah Antun published an article in his own journal, *al-Jāmiʿa* (The Community), in 1902, contending that the lack of tolerance (*tasāmuḥ*) in Islam led Muslims to be hostile towards scholars and scholarship, not only those of other religions, but also of Muslims who held different views, most notably philosophy and philosophers. On the contrary, today's European toleration of science and philosophy attests to Christianity's intellectual

42 ʿImāra, *al-Aʿmāl al-kāmila*, Vol. 1, pp. 225–7.
43 ʿImāra, *al-Aʿmāl al-kāmila*, Vol. 1, pp. 308–9.
44 Scharbrodt, *Muhammad ʿAbduh*, p. 191.
45 ʿImāra, *al-Aʿmāl al-kāmila*, Vol. 3, pp. 308–9.

hospitality, as opposed to Islam's hostility. In addition, Antun invoked Muslim sectarian wars, including those between Sunnites and Shīʿites, and between the ʿAbbāsids and the Umayyads, to support the claim that Islamic history bears witness to his thesis.[46]

In response to those correlations, ʿAbduh provides a counterargument from history, showing how Muslim history includes many philosophers and scientists, both non-Muslim and Muslim, who were not only left alone with their scholarship but were also patronised by various rulers, and in numerous instances held important governmental and scholarly posts, as scientists, teachers, and translators of Greek philosophy and logic.[47] As for the Muslim sectarian conflicts, most prominently Sunnite–Shīʿites, ʿAbduh argued that these were primarily political in nature, not religious; none of them were essentially over creedal matters. Christianity, in contrast, exhibited a much lower degree of tolerance throughout its history. To this end, ʿAbduh invited Antun to consider the sectarian wars that transpired between Protestants and Catholics, and how the Catholic Church persecuted science and scientists, leading to the expulsion of Jews and Muslims from Spain during the Christian Inquisition. In fact, he shows how Europe's advancement is partly due to what they gained from Muslim civilisation in Spain rather than only their own hard work.[48] Otherwise, Muslims exhibited a great sense of tolerance, as shown in his following description:

> A student would move freely from the jurist to sit in front of the philosopher, and from a class of *Ḥadīth* to a class on ethics. If a debate took place on a particular issue, freedom of thought prevailed based on persuasion and a compelling argument, while zealotry diminished within the deliberations and tolerance predominated.

While Scharbrodt and Mahmoud Ayoub categorise ʿAbduh's engagement with Antun as one of apology, it is argued here again that it was rather one of epistemology.[49] Antun makes a scholarly mistake by not only judging

46 Scharbrodt, *Muhammad ʿAbduh*, pp. 191–2.
47 ʿImāra, *al-Aʿmāl al-kāmila*, Vol. 3, pp. 273–5.
48 ʿImāra, *al-Aʿmāl al-kāmila*, Vol. 3, pp. 277–310.
49 Scharbrodt, *Muhammad ʿAbduh*, pp. 191–2; Mahmoud Ayyub, 'Islam and Christianity: A

Christianity by the current state of Christians and Islam by the current state of Muslims, but also by comparing the supposed 'best' of today's Christianity with the 'worst' of Islam. Not only does this constitute a form of reductionism, but also one of anachronism – judging the past from today's perspectives. While one can study Islam through Muslims, with Shahab Ahmad's *What is Islam*? as a case in point, this can barely produce a normative understanding of Islam. Hence, ʿAbduh interrogates such a misreading. What confirms the above is the fact that ʿAbduh never spared earlier and contemporary Muslims from his criticism, either in this work or in his other writings. Indeed, his own criticism of Muslims extended to their contemporary intolerance of differing opinions, their antagonism to modern science, and their sense of intellectual prejudice.[50]

One might object to this reading by saying that ʿAbduh was not critical of Islam per se here, but rather of Muslims, as opposed to his critique of Christianity. Namely, he viewed Christianity itself as being 'irrational, intolerant, and other-worldly', while Islam is viewed as 'rational, tolerant, and finds a better balance between human welfare in this life and in the hereafter'.[51] To this we say, regardless of the correctness or incorrectness of ʿAbduh's conclusions, his mere stepping back to study the two religions in 'essence', not as embodied in their followers or in reducing them to their contemporary realities, makes his attempt one of epistemology, rather than being one of mere apology. This is how ʿAbduh himself saw his own response and hence reminds us of his intention at the end of his engagement, stating:

> Before I leave the reader I want him to note that, in what I summarise in these chapters, there was no intent to criticise an individual or a group, as the reader will know from the form and content of the essays, which are free from polemics, and the avoidance of any words which carry the scent of criticising another. He will know from this avoidance that this is a view that we prepared to nourish ourselves with and that we used it to support those we are responsible for in our community,

Study of Muhammad Abduh's View of the Two Religions', *Humaniora Islamica*, Vol. 2 (1974): 121–37.

50 ʿImāra, *al-Aʿmāl al-kāmila*, Vol. 3, p. 284.

51 Scharbrodt, *Muhammad ʿAbduh*, p. 193.

> and it did not occur to us when we found ourselves preparing it to withhold it from others. Rather, if a night traveller was guided to the light of our fire and requested hospitality from us, we would share with them what is livelier than the spirit of life itself and what is more pleasurable than the ethic of forbearance, if God wills.[52]

A note on the translation

ʿAbduh's poetic prose doubled our task. We needed not only to maintain *what* he wrote, that is, the content, but also *how* he wrote it, that is, the form. Hence, we began our work with a literal translation of the Arabic text to ascertain its original intended meanings. Then, this was followed by a liberal revision of the literal translation, with a view to maintaining the flow of the English language in a way that keeps it as accessible as possible, without compromising the original text's meaning. The original text contains a number of ambiguities, and bears witness to 'Abduh's habit as a writer of paraphrasing ideas as quotations. Wherever it has been possible to do so, we have located the sources for 'Abduh's quotations and identified the authorities he cited, and have attempted to clarify what he had left as ambiguous.

Finally, it is worth noting here as well that despite the existence of several editions of the Arabic text, the basis for the translation here is the edition of al-Manār, which came out in 1902 under the title *al-Islām wa-l-Naṣrāniyya maʿa l-ʿIlm wa-l-Madaniyya* and Muhammad ʿImāra's (d. 2020) *al-Aʿmāl al-kāmila liʾl-imām Muḥammad ʿAbduh* (The Complete Works of Muhammad ʿAbduh, 1993), which does not substantially differ from the former. We chose those editions owing to their better readability and enhanced sense of arrangement.

When rendering Arabic words into English, we have followed the IJMES transliteration system (*International Journal of Middle East Studies*), except in cases where we need to comply with the original sources of direct quotations.

52 ʿImāra, *al-Aʿmāl al-kāmila*, Vol. 3, p. 368.

Islam, Muslims, and Colonialism *in response to Gabriel Hanotaux*

Semitic and Aryan civilisations

I have just read an article by Monsieur Hanotaux that was translated in your newspaper from the newspaper *Le Journal* as an addendum to his prior article.[1]

His prior article and some of his addenda stemmed from his concern over the interests of his country, as he wants to invite his countrymen to consider establishing a guiding principle for their interactions with Muslims who are under their governance or who border them in their own kingdoms. That cannot happen, in his view, without investigating the essence of what makes Muslims different from Christians, and by which they prefer Islamic rule over French rule. Thus, if it is possible to inculcate Muslims with a sense of loyalty to the French and to facilitate a unification between what is established in their hearts [i.e. Islam] with blind submission to French rule, and if the hearts of Muslims could contain the tenets of Islamic belief alongside obedience to all French decrees, no matter how low the rank of the commander is, then it will be correct for the French nation to grant the Muslims the right to remain in the land. Otherwise, it

1 The former French Minister of Foreign Affairs, Gabriel Hanotaux (d. 1944), wrote two articles titled 'L'islām' in the newspaper *Le Journal* in March 1900. He had previously served as the Minister of Foreign Affairs from 1894 to 1898 and later became the editor-in-chief of political affairs at *Le Journal*. For more details, see the Introduction. Also see Ammeke Kateman, *Muhammad 'Abduh and His Interlocutors: Religion in a Globalizing World* (Leiden and Boston: Brill, 2019), pp. 167–73.

will be necessary for them [i.e. the French] to arrange their annihilation or their relocation to another continent.

Therefore, his research led him to investigate the principles of the Islamic faith and to compare it [i.e. Islam] with the Christian religion, or rather, compare it with many religions to which he alludes in his article. Then, he would rule in favour of one of them over the other based on the effects that it has upon its adherents.

As for his aim in conducting this research and wrestling with it, it is nothing but a log to kindle the fire of enmity in the hearts of the French people, which will incite their determination to war against the Muslims so that Monsieur Hanotaux will be to the French nation as that famous monk who incited those famous wars.[2] However, we leave this to him and to his knowledge of his state's power and to his civilisational standing in relation to compassion and humanitarianism, and we direct him towards the intelligence of some of the Muslim youth who know the French language, adorn themselves with the literature of the French people, and are elated at the mere mention of French civilisation!

If Monsieur Hanotaux had not embarked upon criticising a foundation of the faith, I would not have lifted my pen to mention his name. I would have sufficed with taking a lesson and an example – the role of one who considers the conditions of communities and the actions of their leaders; the role of a historian who reads to understand, who understands to know and pass judgement, and who is unconcerned whether the speaker gets it right or wrong. As for his derogation of some foundational principles of the faith, that is what I am targeting with my writing today.

One who looks at the words of Monsieur Hanotaux will immediately see that he is an uncritical imitator in the study of history just as he is in theology and that he has accumulated disparate ideas and lumped them all together in his mind. Then, he cast his pen on those ideas haphazardly to puzzle those among the French people who do not know Islam – which is the majority.

He has spoken excessively of the Aryan civilisation and the Semitic civilisation, the difference between them, that one of them overpowered

2 Peter the Hermit (d. 1115) was a prominent preacher of the First Crusade and a leader of the People's Crusade, which arrived in the East before the main crusading armies.

the other, that the Aryan civilisation is the one which defeated the Semitic civilisation, etc.

The cradle of the Aryan civilisation and its fountainhead is India, which today still adheres to the polytheism which Monsieur Hanotaux adores in most of its forms. However, its adherents are the ones who decided to split those who embraced its beliefs into castes without the possibility of mixing between them – their divisions will continue for as long as the world exists. Included among them are individual members of castes whose religion proclaims their inherent inferiority in terms of intellect, physical attributes, and capabilities, and that they cannot elevate their social status until the end of the world – this is the vast majority of them. Then, there are some who are deemed impure, such that it is not permitted for members of other castes to touch them. The cornerstone of their faith lies in the belief that the world's impermanence makes it inappropriate for Man to focus on worldly matters.

Did these ideas come to those of the Brahmin religion from Semitic civilisation? Even though it only came to know about them in recent times and only appealed to a minority of them, it is obvious to anyone familiar with the Indian subcontinent.

Or, does Monsieur Hanotaux think that the civilisation that the Europeans have reached was brought to them by the early migrants who had travelled from Eastern Aryan lands to the West?

Did those established historical facts not occur to him, nor the barbaric Aryanism that was in Europe, and that science and civilisation did not stem from it but came from its interactions with Semitic nations, as is known to anyone who reads Ancient Greek history – and they are the other teachers of Europeans – as Monsieur Hanotaux claims?

What was the Aryan civilisation that was in Europe when the Muslims shrank its borders? Does he mean the mutual shedding of blood and the proclamation of war between science and religion, and between revelation and reason? Certainly, this is what was firmly established among Westerners upon the emergence of Islam.

What did Islam bring to Europe? And what was the civilisation that it brought to them, and they rejected? It brought to them the beneficial arts of the Persians and the Aryan inhabitants of Asia; it brought to them the sciences of the Persians, Egyptians, Romans, and Greeks; it refined and purified all of it from the dirt and debris that had gathered at the hands of rulers of Western nations at that time. They made it clean and pure, radiating for the eyes of the negligent and bewildered who were in the darkness of ignorance, uncertain where they were heading.

I am only giving Monsieur Hanotaux a general account, the details of which are not unknown to his people and many fair-minded among them must acknowledge.

The first spark that ignited the hearts of Westerners and carried them towards modern civilisation came from that burning fire whose light spread from Al-Andalus to the surrounding regions. Many men of the Christian faith tried for centuries to put it out but were unable to find a way to do so. Today, the people of Europe graze on what has grown in their own lands after it was irrigated by the blood of their ancestors, shed by the hands of their own faith leaders who were driven by their hostility towards science, freedom, and all signs of modern civilisation.

The reader will be confused by Monsieur Hanotaux's understanding of the Semitic civilisation that Islam brought that clashed with Aryan civilisation. Perhaps his concern for historical nomenclature alongside his inability to penetrate the reality that those terms contain are what prevented his success in foreign policy with nations such as the French, which wisely entrusts its leadership to intelligent individuals. For someone cognisant of the innate characteristics of nations, guiding them toward the path that secures their victory over neighbouring nations would not pose a challenge, but it is incredibly difficult to find someone who has that level of insight today.

Anyone who gazes into the annals of the past will have his eyes filled red with the imagery of bloodshed spanning the epochs – blood that was shed by adherents of that faith which associates itself with Aryan civilisation [i.e. Christians] to resist the advocates of that Semitic civilisation [i.e. Muslims] and to extinguish its fire.

Were it possible to make reliable assessments of religions by considering the conditions of their adherents as observed at the time of judgement, then we can judge that there is no connection between the Christian faith and modern civilisation. The Gospel is in our hands for us to read and understand; none of its intricate meaning is lost on us. The Gospel commands its followers to separate themselves from the temporal world and remain austere within it. If a thief steals their coat they are obligated to also give him their cloak, and if one strikes their right cheek they are to turn the left cheek to them also.[3] Also, they must dedicate themselves entirely to the Father, and the Gospel narrates to them that it is easier for a camel to pass through the eye of a needle than for a wealthy person to enter the Kingdom of God.[4] Likewise, there are heavenly pieces of advice which are fitting for a divine messenger who invites mankind to abstain from this temporal world to be permitted to join the people of the everlasting world.

Did it ever occur to Monsieur Hanotaux to make 'Render to Caesar the things that are Caesar's and to God the things that are God's' a principle, as advised by the Gospel? Does he see an equivalent for that in the Aryan civilisation, which established a bond of sisterhood with the Christian faith?

Eye-witness observation tells us that nothing of the kind took place. Instead, this civilisation was characterised by monarchs and rulers, gold and silver, ostentation and pomp, deception and hypocrisy; its ultimate authority is the pound for some and the lira for others – the Gospel had no say whatsoever.

The Messiah taught rendering to Caesar the things that are Caesar's so that Christians would not rebel against their non-Christian kings. However, this principle has been inverted such that they are unable to even tolerate having non-Christian subjects, let alone non-Christian kings.

Yes, there are people today who uphold the commandments of the Gospel, a group of Americans who have left their land, homes, and wealth, and arrived in Jerusalem waiting for the descent of the Messiah to welcome him as soon as he arrives upon the famous pulpit so that they would be first to kiss his hands and feet. They are pure-hearted, of clear conscience, and without greed in so far as they have abstained from all works other than studying the Bible. If this was the Aryan civilisation that Islam fought against then I would be the first to concede to his arguments and be convinced by his proofs.

From among the Semites are the Phoenicians, who taught them agriculture and trade, let alone reading and writing. Also, from among them are the Aramaeans, who had an undeniable civilisation in the days of

3 See King James Bible, Matthew 5:39–40.
4 See King James Bible, Matthew 19:24.

Rome, nor would contemporary Westerners deny their merit in that regard. Indeed, the foundational principles of agriculture and trade are shared by all nations ascending the ladder of humanity. People only differ from one another in accordance with what life's necessities shape within them, what the cloud of adversity rains down upon them, and by what different environments impress upon them. Nations have always learnt civilisation from one another, with no difference between an Aryan and a Semite, whenever they feel the need to adopt an innovation, a resource, or a field of knowledge to avert one of life's difficulties or to fine-tune a matter.

The Aryan West learnt more from the Semitic East than what the diminishing East of today is acquiring from the self-reliant West. Accordingly, all that remains from the essence of civilisation which the author intended is faith. It is clear from his words that the essence of Semitic faith is monotheism, and the essence of Aryan faith is the opposite.

I can confirm for this famous minister an obvious truth that is known to preschool children: monotheistic faith is not a Semitic religion but is a Hebrew one which was defined by Abraham, peace be upon him, and his offspring; among them is Jesus from his mother's side and his companions and early disciples. As for the remaining Semites – Arabs, Phoenicians, Aramaeans, and others mentioned in the Bible that are known to him – they were commonly known as polytheists and anthropomorphists. In that they did not differ from their cousins, or even their so-called foes, the Aryans.

The author has dealt with the precedence that anthropomorphism and corporealisation have over God's unicity and has mentioned causes and reasons for that, aided by his vast knowledge of philosophy and the social sciences. We will elaborate upon this as it is the aim of our essay, by God's will.

Before putting pen to paper, I remind those who devote themselves to praising the likes of this minister – just as Muslims devote themselves to God, in his view – that if I downplay Hanotaux's expertise in historical knowledge it is because he truly is a novice in the field, and many of his compatriots are aware of that about him, because the only true master in knowledge is knowledge itself. Regards.

Hanotaux on predestination and transcendence

Monsieur Hanotaux has found fault with two issues that are among the major foundations of the faith: predestination and God's absolute unity, or transcendence. After falling short in explaining the problems associated with the first issue, and people's historically different views about it, and that they belong to two groups: those who say that humans are not endowed with free will and cannot choose their actions, and those who say that their Creator endowed them with free will and they will be compensated for their good and evil acts, he said: 'The first view places man at the lowest levels of weakness whereas the second raises him to the apex of strength.' Then, he connected the first to the Buddhists who affirmed the annihilation of all existent things into an eternal existence, and the second to the ancient Greeks who anthropomorphised God with man in his tangible attributes. He said that the first view demotes its adherents whereas the second promotes them to the lofty ranks of perfection. This represents a level of confusion and arbitrariness that is unmatched.

Then, he set on to the two religions: Christianity and Islam. He said that they embody those two views (i.e. the two views on predestination). The first are those who inherited from the Aryans and the second from the Semites. The first raises mankind to a divine level whereas the second lowers them to the animalistic level. The inclination of both religions is plainly apparent in the principle that they have each used as a foundation. The principle of the former is that the Divine Father created the Divine Son – so there is a divine human – and both are connected to the Holy Spirit. The principle of the latter is divine transcendence to the extent that the relation between God and mankind is severed.

He then returns to mixing the two religions, reducing them to a single principle, drawing comparisons between the two, and the rest of what he futilely elaborates upon.

Has there ever been a case of muddled thinking or verbal deficiency among authors and individuals of insight in a way that compares to the writing of this author? I will leave judgement of that for anyone who has the slightest level of familiarity with the thoughts and viewpoints held by various nations.

The issue of predestination is not confined to a single group, anthropomorphists or those who affirm God's transcendence, as those two issues have nothing to do with this matter. Rather, the genesis of this debate in theology is God's omniscience and omnipotence – whether God's knowledge encompasses everything and whether there is an extension of His power to all possibilities. The dispute among Christians themselves in this matter was significant, and they are anthropomorphists in Monsieur Hanotaux's view. The debate between them started before Islam and continues until the present day. Perhaps Hanotaux could study Thomists – followers of Saint Thomas Aquinas (d. 1274) – or the Dominicans, as they are all determinists, and the Jesuits who are libertarians. Each of these views has representative groups among the Christian denominations and it is not a Semitic issue, as he claims. Rather, its roots sprouted and its branches grew among the Aryans, and then their contagion spread to others.

Have you heard of a Jew lying flat on his back, abandoning all action while relying solely upon predestination? Have you heard of a single Phoenician – whose rowboats had reached the British Isles – who slept and indulged in his dreams depending solely on what the unseen would lead him to? Yet, we have heard of this in monasteries and among the friars, and we know stories of numerous individuals who relied solely on the support of others until Europe reached a point where it raised an outcry against them and demanded their forceful removal.

The school of philosophy among the Greeks that argued for chance and arbitrariness became well-known and is even familiar to novices in philosophy; the refutation of this is the starting point of philosophical literature. It is the view of those who contend that things exist due to chance or non-contingence and that which is possible does not require a reason to exist. Is this not more worthy of belonging to Determinism than attributing all matters to the Creator of the universe? Does this school really elevate its Aryan proponent to attaining a high standing and a place of honour?

The Qur'ān – the revealed scripture of Islam – censures and rebukes determinists. It critiques their statement: 'If God had willed, we would not have ascribed partners to Him – nor would our fathers – or have declared anything forbidden,' by saying: 'in the same way, those before them continually denied [the truth] until they tasted Our punishment. Say, "Have you any knowledge that you can show us? You follow only supposition and tell only lies.'"[5] It affirms the doctrine of man's acquisition of his acts and of free choice in almost sixty-four verses. Anything which it mentions that could cause one to imagine the opposite of that was only mentioned to affirm the general Divine habit, known as the universal laws of nature, as in the verse: 'If God had so willed, He would have made you one community,' and other comparable passages.[6]

An intelligent person can see the clear difference between an individual's free choice in their actions and an indication of Divine predeterminism, for example, in the matter of temperaments and setting of natural dispositions. One's sentiments are established by the choices he makes in his actions and only one who is ignorant of his own self denies this. But as for the differing natures, traits, and dispositions of communities, no creature of God has any choice in that. Moreover, his createdness is like the creation of the heavens and the earth and everything between them.

The Prophet, peace and blessings upon him, supported that with his words and actions; he was an untiring worker, indefatigably industrious, vigilant without rest, and incomparably hardworking. Do you say about him that he ever laid his head upon his pillow and surrendered to predestination in completing his mission, saying that the one who guaranteed him victory freed him from having to make any effort and that God's guarantee to elevate His religion's word spared him from exertion? Never. Rather, the true divine promises only increased his energy and the divine infallibility afforded to him only served to increase his determination and precaution.

His companions followed his example and they in turn were followed by the early *Salaf*.[7] They of all people had the most complete faith in God's omniscience and omnipotence and were the most knowledgeable regarding the value of reason and free choice that God had endowed them with. They were the epitome of hard work and were exemplars of perseverance and man's acquisition, such that what they bequeathed in their efforts to spread Islam still pains Hanotaux and his likes today.

---

5 Qur'ān 6:148. For translations of Qur'anic verses throughout these essays, please see M.A.S. Abdel Haleem, *The Qur'an: A New Translation* (Oxford: Oxford World's Classics, 2008).

6 Qur'ān 5:48.

7 Predecessors or ancestors, though usually used with the meaning of 'pious ancestors' in reference to the first three generations of the Muslim community.

This is the Semitic creed or the Muhammadan call or the Islamic civilisation! It elevated its proponents, when they were Bedouins inhabiting distant places of the earth; they did not get to partake in the delights of civilisation nor savour the fruits of knowledge and craftsmanship until it reached the heights through their endeavours, ultimately securing the seat of power and authority. Then, with it, they attained a level of sensitivity and pure intellect which enabled them to win over other communities such that the progeny of those Bedouins learned things that were previously unknown to them and unveiled that which had been hidden from them and extracted the treasures of their knowledge, the benefit of which became apparent to the Europeans a number of centuries after the Prophetic mission.

Alas! The egos of certain Muslim leaders were inflated in a manner akin to prideful devils and they took up the scum from the filth of the Aryans and polluted the pure earth and contaminated its surface; its impurity proliferated and its contemptibility spread extensively.

Then came the Persian and Roman *mawāli* donning the attire of the Islamic faith while importing their own controversies and hypocrisy.[8] They introduced the innovation of disputation in creedal matters and disobeyed God and His messenger's prohibition of delving into the question of predestination. They misled the Muslims with empty sayings and crooked words until they split into factions. God had told His prophet: 'As for those who have divided their religion and broken up into factions, have nothing to do with them [Prophet].'[9]

There was a group among the Muslims known as the *Jabriyya* (Rejectors of Free-will), but they were weak and insignificant. Truth disowned them, intellect rejected them, and faith abandoned them, such that they disappeared soon after their emergence and they did not remain as the Thomists did among the Christians. However, the school of reconciling predestination and free will gained prominence among Muslims and it is a school of resolve, effort, and true faith, and it was adopted from the Muslims much later by insightful Christians, such as Beaussier (d. 1873) and those who followed him. The vast majority of Christians then followed them.

8 Non-Arab Muslims, but also used to refer to clients of Arab tribes.

9 Qur'ān, 6:159.

However, I do not dispute that time turned its back on the Muslims, just as it did to others, and they were tested by some corrupt Sufis for many centuries who spread delusions which had no relation to the foundations of their faith.[10] These delusions were ingrained in their minds not as articles of creed but as demonic goading which seized the unlearned and perplexed the learned, unless they contained the mechanisms of sound faith. Lethargy developed among Muslims due to the spread of ignorance about the principles of their faith. This was supported by the inclinations of their leaders to become involved in this, as is their wont in all nations.

It is worth mentioning that this type of Sufism is also one of the remnants of the Aryans, as it came to us from the Persians and Indians who retained their initial creedal beliefs.

Nothing misled Hanotaux and his like into having such short-sightedness more than those pernicious dervishes or the feeble-minded who have covered the ends of Algeria and Tunis, and no region of Islam today is free of those who have taken their faith as a means of trade whereby they acquire the vanities of the world and those who have made a tool of God's remembrance by which they usurp the wealth of the common folk.

If Muslims returned to the essence of their faith they would fulfil their obligations, cause their lands to prosper, and increase their wealth, they would be ready for France with all of the strength they could muster and would firmly depend upon the backing of God's order for their success. They would have had firm faith knowing that there is no escape from death, and then they would have attacked their most honoured position and would have taken that which the strong take from the weak and the noble take from the ignoble – their madness, as characterised by Hanotaux, would have been reason and their delirium would have become knowledge and wisdom.

This is what relates to his feeble opinion on the issue of predestination for Muslims. As for the issue of anthropomorphisation and transcendentalisation, we will give it its due right in the epilogue of this essay to spare the reader any boredom. Regards.

10 Such anti-Sufi statements have often, and mistakenly so, been understood as a sheer rejection of Sufism. However, this is a critique only of certain strands of Sufism. Otherwise, ʿAbduh speaks positively of Sufism and its contribution to what he achieved in his intellectual and spiritual life. See Rashīd Riḍā, *Tārīkh al-imām Muḥammad ʿAbduh*, 2nd edn, Vol. 1 (Cairo: Dār al-Faḍīla, 2006), pp. 26; 108; 126–30.

Transcendence vs anthropomorphism

Today I bring the final word to shatter Hanotaux's malice in his attack on Islam. That which I intend to speak about today is the affirmation of God's unicity and transcendentalisation as opposed to anthropomorphisation and corporealisation. I will begin by speaking about the latter and then conclude by discussing the former.

If Monsieur Hanotaux had read and understood a single thing about human societies and the development of creeds, he would know that polytheism and pantheism were the beliefs of those who stood at the gates of humanity and did not enter it nor did they reach its peaks; such views were and still are an indication of the intellectual decline of its proponents, with variations in this decline, starting with the polytheists of Africa and ending with the Buddhists of China and the Brahmins of India.

However, the more Man advanced in knowledge, refined his intuition through understanding, and set his mind free for contemplation of the secrets of the universe, the veils of materialism were torn in front of him, and the Highest Existent was revealed to him with variations in the clarity of His manifestation, leading him to the belief in one Necessary Existent which it is impossible to materialise in the way that Monsieur Hanotaux and his like assume, for that which has no limit cannot be contained by boundaries.

This was the state of the Greeks, in whose civilisation Hanotaux takes pride. They emerged as polytheists, but polytheism shrank and died with their progress in various sciences and the research of their philosophers into the nature of existences until they arrived, whilst at the pinnacle of their civilisation, at monotheism and the transcendence of the Necessary Existent from mixing with matter.

Pythagoras stood at the threshold of transcendentalisation. Socrates, Plato, and Aristotle came after him, working diligently to remove the veils from the eyes of their nation, trying with all their might to remove the darkness of the initial polytheism which had enveloped the souls of their people. Anyone who reads Plato's *The Republic* – which was translated into Arabic as 'The Ideal City' during the reign of Al-Ma'mūn (r. 813–833) – will know how Plato fought against the ridiculous beliefs and reprehensible practices that endured as remnants of polytheism that prevented the Greek nations from taking on the virtues which the philosopher wished for them to adopt.

Once knowledge enabled them to arrive at monotheism, transcendentalisation did not cause them to fall back into ignorance. On the contrary, the sun of their civilisation illuminated the world for many centuries, casting the brightest and most radiant light.

Such was also the case with the ancient Egyptians. Knowledge made them affirm monotheism, although the leaders of their faith did not propagate that belief among the masses. Rather, they maintained the forms of their initial ritual worship and wrapped transcendentalisation in the attire of anthropomorphisation as a way to monopolise the nobility of that belief.

Thus, you see that a weak intellect, lack of knowledge, and poor comprehension lead one to pause at intermediaries, whereas a strong intellect, penetrating insight, and comprehensive knowledge raise one to the sight of the Highest Existent, causing one to rise above the entire world and see it in its entirety, the lofty and the base, as equal in its relation to that comprehensive power and grand majesty. All of that emanates from the inception of existence and gets divided into ranks, in accordance with a wise arrangement that is perfected by divine favour.

What rank could be higher than the rank of one who affirms this belief, such that he can bear witness before the entire universe, with his subtle understanding and complete comprehension, concluding that it is all under the lordship of a single Lord, who is the Lord of all existence, and nothing within it has any authority to create or sustain? Rather, he alone is able, via the divine law that He established for him (i.e. Man), to arrive at that divine presence and attain support from it in all his affairs.

Proponents of anthropomorphisation can be divided into two camps: one believes that divine power lies in certain creatures and then stops at them, and the other believes that the Creator of existence manifests in some of them.

As for the former, they are those whose comprehension is too weak to comprehend the truths of existence. If the strength of a powerful entity or the might of an animal is made apparent to them, they consider it to have sole power over them and they rely upon it in all of their matters. These people grant authority over themselves to whatever they and their ignorance want – statues, animals, and people. They remain perplexed about their lives just as they are about their objects of worship. They measure their objects of worship against themselves as they are not dissimilar in category or type; they presume wants and desires for them which exceed their own, and they compete with one another to please them as their desires have dictated to them.

As such, grave offences have been committed in their temples and limits of virtue have been transgressed in their sanctuaries; human sacrifices are offered to stone statues. Is there a lower level that Man has fallen to than this? It has been a known phenomenon throughout history and remains known to be witnessed right up to today.

As for the latter, they have a higher level of comprehension than the former. However, what have they attained through this belief? If someone exceeds them in intellect or bravery, or he accomplishes an unprecedented feat, or he presents something to them that they are unfamiliar with, they think God manifests himself in him. As a result, they surrender their authority to him, yield to his power, and humble themselves according to his will. Thus, he seizes all the intellect, will, and determination that they possess. They deserve lowliness for as long as they remain in that creed.

This delusion has enabled many people of cunning to attain ranks of divinity among the masses, seeking to enslave them. How many heavy losses have nations endured which were brought upon them by these misguided beliefs?

Similar to these is a third category which is no better than the first two: those who believe in intermediaries. They have no grasp of God's true measure, so they measure him against their leaders and aristocracy and assume that He in his kingship is similar to a worldly king in his tyranny, choosing leaders from among His creation and creating workers to have free reign in the affairs of his worshippers. If one of them distinguishes himself by drawing close to God, according to their beliefs, or he performs a feat which they assume to be proof that he is one of God's chosen elect, they raise him to that station – the station of predisposition to act freely in the universe. Thus, they take him as an intercessor to God and seek his support in their important matters, asking for his help due to his closeness to God. If they are asked about this and about their beliefs, they respond: 'We worship them only so they may bring us closer to God.'[11]

11 Qur'ān 39:3.

What have these people gained by their beliefs? They were subjugated by the sacristan, the soothsayer, and the leaders and those who followed them; they surrendered all of their affairs to them. Their sciences were, in fact, delusions, and their comprehension only corresponded to their imaginations. They denied first principles if they presumed they contradicted those delusions which they acquired from their leaders. Then they abandoned all practical means of attaining eminence, instead relying upon those they asked for help. History still acts as a witness to the misfortunes of these beliefs that humanity endured and eye-witness testimony supports it with many of the Western and Eastern communities until today.

These are the depravities of polytheism and its like. No one who has studied the foundational principles of sound knowledge denies this. Moreover, even many of the unlearned masses who were not raised in the midst of its foul atmosphere know it.

As for Hanotaux's claim that Greek polytheism elevated the Greeks on the moral ladder, hoping to attain divine rank, it is a claim that no other Christian other than he has made, as far as I know, and the Greeks themselves never stated they were striving to attain virtues via connection to the divine station, nor that divine humanity had a desirable effect upon them. Rather, it only left them with those depravities which Socrates and Plato contested. As for striving for virtues, it was simply to draw closer to their deities, as is known.

As for his verdict on Christianity, that it stems from the faith of the ancient Greeks, I will leave commenting upon that for the Christians themselves. However, I will say that Christianity tried with all its might, in its earliest stages, to cleanse the earth of the polytheism that people followed during its time and opposed anyone – Romans and Jews – who tarnished its beliefs, and its adherents spread among the polytheists to invite them to monotheism. God's transcendence was the basis of their invitation, as anyone who closely studies their words knows, and there was no trace of anthropomorphism in them until many centuries later; the history of the Byzantine Empire is known to people of knowledge and there is no need to go into detail about it.

Then, as there was exaggeration regarding anthropomorphism, iniquities appeared, damages increased, knowledge declined, rationality was driven away, the pillars of order crumbled, and corruption worsened among

Christian communities until the Reformation appeared and did away with what came before it so that Europe was set right upon its known path. We have alluded to some of the reasons for that.

We have never heard of a single Christian worshipping God to attain the rank of the Messiah such that he becomes a divine human, as can be understood from Hanotaux's wording. Furthermore, we have not seen any sign that any of them understood the doctrine of the Trinity in the manner that he mentioned. Rather, they state that it is a doctrine that has no room for rational inquiry, so he is unable to emulate it. Throughout the ages, certain denominations have clearly stated that there is a difference between that which is beyond the realm of rationality, and that which contradicts rationality, and they have held the view that the Messiah was only a chosen prophet that God sent to save mankind from Satan's hold. They interpreted 'the Son' to mean 'the Chosen' and 'the Father' to mean 'the Merciful Lord.'[12] I know some of the Protestant denominations today, though they are few in number, who interpret 'the Logos' as 'Knowledge' and 'the Holy Spirit' as 'Life.' I met some of them during my travels and they assured me that they have a group which believes in that.

In bygone times, did Christianity fight the polytheists around them merely to expel them from one form of polytheism into another? We seek refuge in God from this confusion issued by a non-scholar devotee. It is not befitting for me to criticise Christian doctrine in a newspaper, as I have been commanded to argue in the most courteous way.[13] However, I will return to commenting upon the points that Hanotaux used as evidence.

Islam came to invite the whole world to monotheism. It stated that the religion of transcendentalisation is the religion of God from Adam, Noah, and Abraham to Moses. Then it is the religion of the prophets after Moses and the religion of the final prophet from the Tribes of Israel, Jesus. He did not deny that among the Jews, and especially among the Christians, were proponents of transcendentalisation, and he mentioned that some of them were inclined towards anthropomorphisation. He called on them to return to the original faith so that they could worship God alone and be

12 'It seems probable that 'Abduh refers to nineteenth-century Unitarianism here; a Christian (Protestant) movement that denies the Trinity and affirms that God is one.' See Kateman, *Muhammad 'Abduh and His Interlocutors*, p. 190.

13 Reference to Qur'ān 16:125.

freed from the authority of their rulers and leaders who had usurped their rationality and taken control of their desires and interests.

Polytheism, Judaism, and Christianity attempted to oppose Islam, and they had greater numbers, superior strength, and intense resolve. Before long, the truth became manifest and its light pierced hearts causing individuals from all religious backgrounds to join the faith in droves; ambitions were unshackled, aspirations were wholly set loose, and each pursued perfection in accordance with their preparedness which was bestowed to them by the Necessary Existent. Believers in monotheism and transcendentalisation observed from the pinnacle of faith the secrets of existence and they tore those veils and delusions and directly connected to the sources of knowledge – thought, inquiry, and faith. The people of this way did not relent from this prosperous dissension until the light of knowledge shone within them, and there remained no door they had not entered, no height they had not scaled, and they extracted all remnants of the Greeks, Persians, and Romans from forgotten corners, dusted them off, and made them attractive to behold.

This is the effect of Islam, the religion of transcendentalisation. The second century after its appearance had barely ended when the Muslims occupied themselves with the field of astronomy. They corrected errors, refined principles, fixed foundations, and, at the beginning of the third century, they established observatories and surveyed the Earth. In doing so, they introduced concepts and practices that are now commonplace among scientists in our land and the land of Monsieur Hanotaux.

I will be content in this matter with the words of a group of researchers in Western nations today: 'Christianity had been around for sixteen centuries without producing a single astronomer, whereas the Muslims began their investigations in this field in a matter of years after the death of their Prophet.'[14]

Nonetheless, this is not a criticism of the foundations of Christianity, but a criticism of the actions of those who follow it and have changed it from its original message.

Hanotaux thinks that Islam severs the tie between God and worshipper, but he has erred in that. Islam leads the worshipper to his Lord and

14 Here and elsewhere, it has been impossible to identify the exact source for these quotations. See comment on page xxxi.

makes it his right to stand before Him alone without an intermediary. Islam has decreed for there to be only one overwhelming power in the universe which every being owes their devotion to. It has prohibited mankind from reaching two stations which they cannot attain: the station of divinity that is specific to Him and the station of prophethood which He chooses to grant to whom He wills and then He closes its doors. As for the remaining steps of human perfection, they are in front of mankind and are attainable with no barrier, except one's own shortcomings, in action or contemplation.

If you believe that God has shown little favour to you then you will have hindered yourself and you will be unable to find a way to progress. This is how true Islam raises the spirit of its adherents, and this is the meaning of Islam and submission, which Monsieur Hanotaux misunderstands. With this meaning of Islam, does humanity remain at the animalistic level and does it renounce the link between causes and effects in attaining virtues and perfection?

One who researches Islam must investigate its scripture in as much as he looks at its effects; Islam is Islam and Muslims are Muslims. If Monsieur Kimon, whom Hanotaux cites, had smelt the fragrance of knowledge he would not have regurgitated such filth, and there is no need to comment on this as his imbecilic opinions and lack of character suffice.[15]

How did this happen to Muslims? How were their creeds penetrated by anthropomorphism and how were their practices afflicted with insincerity? From whom did they learn rapacity and from whom did they acquire evil desires? I know the answer to that as do all educated people, and God encompasses them from all sides.

Muslims have entirely mirrored those who came before them and reached identical outcomes. They have exchanged comparable misconceptions and have been drawn into identical situations, encountering the same challenges. There have been heresies in the faith that have destroyed

15 This is in reference to D. Kimon's book *La pathologie de l'islam* in which the author advocates the need to destroy Islam by annihilating one-twentieth of the world's Muslim population and subjecting the rest to a regime of semi-slavery until they finally convert to Catholicism. See Fernando Bravo López 'The Genocidal Islamophobia of a Late Nineteenth-Century French Anti-Semite: D. Kimon and the Pathology of Islam', *Islam and Christian–Muslim Relations*, Vol. 25, No. 1 (2014): 101–16.

virtues and decimated the crème de la crème, leading Muslims to be targets for the likes of Kimon.

But if Muslims were to return to the Qur'ān and, in following it, regain those lost etiquettes, they would be free from blame and would seek the means of felicity that their scripture and their prophet guide them towards, and that was prepared for them by the greats of old. Power would be consolidated for them and the spirit of nobility would pervade them. Then, what Hanotaux and Kimon will have to face of this faith when it is authentic will be much more dangerous for them than what they fear of it when it is distorted with heresies.

Kimon is of the opinion that Islam and Muslims should be wiped from the face of the earth. Hanotaux sees the validity of this view, though he does not go all the way owing to the large number of Muslims. What a poor choice of politics for ruling their lands, exposing their vileness, and bringing to light their foolish opinions and poor judgement.

They and anyone else who deceives themselves like them should know that Islam, if it has a prolonged absence, will return, and if breaches have caused damage, there will be a resurgence. The fair-minded of the English, such as Isaac Taylor (d. 1901) the famous priest and head of his Church, has stated:

> It spread throughout Africa and virtuosity would spread along with it, such that nobility, magnanimity, chivalry, are some of its effects; bravery and courage are some of its supporters.

He deeply regrets the drunkenness and immorality that spread among natives with the spread of evangelism and he stated: 'I choose an Islam which prohibits drunkenness over a Christianity which does not.'[16]

It continues to spread in China and throughout Africa, and circumstances will steer it toward the route of rediscovering its purity and afflictions will

16 These two quotations seem to be paraphrased from Canon Isaac Taylor, 'Christianity and Mohammedanism' quoted in 'Christian Lectures on Buddhism, and Plain Facts about the Same, by Buddhists', *Lucifer* Vol. 2, No. 8 (April 1888): 142–9. Taylor is quoted as saying 'Islam, above all, is the most powerful total abstinence society in the world; whereas the extension of European trade means the extension of drunkenness and vice and the degradation of the people.'

return it to its original genesis. At that time, nations will get to hugely benefit from it, by God's will.

If the French nation were to embrace Islam altogether, with Monsieur Hanotaux at the forefront, but its interactions with the non-French were what we are familiar with in Algeria and Madagascar, do you expect the inhabitants of its colonies to incline towards it and not seize opportunities to revolt? Never. How much more should Muslims then revolt against them, when they hear the roar of this thunder and only see an effort by their conquerors to destroy them and an eagerness to wipe them out?

Justice, the upholding of rights and respect for the beliefs of others, after knowing their principles, are what soften the authority of the conqueror over the conquered, draw him nearer to him, and facilitate contentment with him. But Hanotaux and the other French leaders like him do not know anything about these three principles and they continue to speak nonsensically until that which they had not taken into account appears to them. Thus, let them wait; we are also waiting.

Addressing Hanotaux's critique of Muslim realities

Dear Sir, editor of the noble *al-Mu'ayyad* newspaper

I was surprised by two copies of a well-known newspaper in Egypt which included a conversation between the editor and Monsieur Hanotaux, a man of known hostility against Islam.

I do not doubt that much of the conversation is the view of Monsieur Hanotaux as it could only have come from someone, like him, who knows the circumstances in Europe and many of the circumstances in the East. Therefore, I believe ignoring his views without engaging with them is unfair to him and an injustice against him, particularly given that his being the proponent of such views will leave an effect in the minds of people that cannot be left without comment.

His words are indicative of a poor understanding of the state of Muslims and their interests today. Indeed, poor understanding is the cause of much of the disputation that occurs between people of the same goal, as he himself mentioned in his previous article. Thus, it would not befit one who has a sense of protectiveness over the truth to not educate him. I hope that *al-Mu'ayyad* newspaper will translate what I write here into French and send it to Monsieur Hanotaux so he can be aware of our aims and thoughts.

If Muslims of today can find benefit in anything and take it as a lesson, there will be nothing more beneficial for them than taking heed of what Monsieur Hanotaux has stated, as he has pointed out their undeniable faults and opened their eyes to the objectives of the colonisers in their lands, the effects of which they have seen with their own eyes. He has made it clear that a dependence upon equity in international relations is a type of delusion and expecting justice from such communities is borderline impossible. One who wishes to protect his honour and aims to remain free from blame must think and act like them (i.e. his colonisers) in order to attain their might and exceed their power, or be like them so that he may able to challenge them equally in acquiring gains, rather than using pretexts, and entertaining delusions, and contenting himself with a loud voice and elegant speech that does not originate from the soul of the one who says it, until they attack him when he is in a state of heedlessness and subjugate him while he is either awake or asleep. He will then stretch out his hand seeking their mercy, hoping for some justice coming from their side – such is the attitude of the foolish ignorant. Indeed, he is more deserving of enslavement.

It is advice from non-Muslims that a Muslim must accept, and, before accepting it, he must accept it from Abū Bakr al-Ṣiddīq (r. 632–34), as he said to Khālid ibn al-Walīd (d. 642) when he sent him to the Battle of Yamāma: 'Fight them as they fight you: sword against sword and spear against spear.'

It is obvious that every dispute is, in essence, a battle; competing to attain that which life depends upon is the essence of conflict; any action taken by one of the competitors to win the competition is an act of aggression; all means of attaining victory are the weapons; the give and take between them is the confrontation; every advantage held or extracted is plunder; and all forsaking of rights or denial of benefit is defeat.

The victor on the battlefield is the one whose mind is more cunning, whose prowess is stronger, and whose weapons are sharper. If the two sides are evenly matched it is possible for them to reach an agreement in which they both benefit. If not, an agreement will be impossible and only the stronger will benefit. Moreover, it will be difficult for the weaker side even to attain the right to not be eradicated. This is God's habit in this temporal world.

Monsieur Hanotaux has detailed that which was summarised by some of our teachers in his words: 'Justice is proportional to strength.'

Monsieur Hanotaux has stated that Europe was only concerned with internal matters prior to being driven to colonial enterprises and that the only thing that could repel them was the power of the nations they wanted to colonise. He gives the example of Japan: as it advanced in civilisation, reformed its internal affairs, and prepared to protect its sovereignty, it proclaimed its strength to Europe and compelled it to recognise its standing. Thus, Japan protected its own land and property from attack, and demonstrating its power allowed it to unite its own goals with those of the Europeans. This is true, and the Muslims should have known it for centuries as their scripture is the best source of guidance – a single verse suffices: 'Prepare whatever forces you can muster.'[17] This noble verse calls them to preparation and demands they do so to the limits of their capabilities, and there are no limits once a nation is able to use all of its physical and intellectual prowesses in the manner it was made to do, and so its strength is unleashed, which is all that one can do against opposition and, thereby, be capable of protecting one's life and property from the aggression of an enemy, or at least protecting one's rights from the hand of a usurper. The best form of strength is that which preserves the truth and increases benefit such that both sides stop in awe at its limits so that peace can be established between them and they can each be content with their lot.

The power of European nations is comprised of certain elements: knowledge, literature, trade, industry, justice, religion, and arms. I mentioned religion within the list as Monsieur Hanotaux would not deny that Europe has depended on religion in managing colonialism. Religious missionaries and organisations are among the most important means of preparing local communities to accept their authority when the opportunity presents itself for that and to ready the people to condone whatever that authority decrees for them, as long as it falls within their remit. Also, they are needed for untying knots which no arms could alone untie and for creating pathways that no army officer could himself create. These are accepted matters

17 Qur'ān 8:60.

that no one who has any knowledge of the matter, like Hanotaux, would dispute. Therefore, there is no need to go into detail on this, though I will mention an incident which I witnessed myself, and there is no problem with mentioning it here.

A young man from Mount Lebanon, in Syria, studied in one of the French evangelical schools in that region and studied literature with his teachers, reading a number of their authors' publications. His heart was filled with a love of France and his mind settled on the idea that it is the beacon of knowledge and freedom, and that it would free the entire world from the bondage of despotism. Then, he busied himself with the books of French philosophers and the works of some of their politicians until his belief grew that it was important for the administration of this great nation to spread its knowledge around the world to train hearts and minds and educate them about the principles of rationality and free thought. He thought that it would draw him closer to them if he went to Paris to the French government and asked for help in building schools in Mount Lebanon in which the curriculums could be based upon those aforementioned principles. Consequently, he went to Paris in 1884 and networked with an intelligent Syrian who had good standing in France, asking him to facilitate the attainment of the government support he desired. The man did his part and then returned to his friend, saying to him: 'What you have thought up is a type of delusion. The French government, despite having expelled the Jesuits from their land and opposing the authority of their church – their foreign administration is purely religious, as can be seen from their protection of the Jesuits and their financial and military support for them in your land. You are more likely to have success if you want to open religious schools in Lebanon. Otherwise, go back and work on something that suits your own needs.'

The young man left disappointed after he had been there for some time and spent all his money. He could not find anyone who would help him return to his land until some of our friends helped him, and I myself had a hand in helping him and was a witness to the conversation I have just related.

If Muslims do not try with earnest conviction to attain those elements which were mentioned or to strengthen those they already have but which have weakened, they will be contradicting their own scripture and the saying of al-Ṣiddīq, God be pleased with him. They would deserve the blame of Monsieur Hanotaux and there would be no way for their interests to unite equally with those of the Europeans until Judgement Day.

I still need to address two issues with this statesman:

1. His understanding of the state of Muslims today, and that which they refer to as a call to unite the Muslim cause without exception and combine political and religious authority in one person.
2. Muslims' ill assumptions about European politicians, or rather, all Christians, such that they have lost confidence in them to the extent that they do not trust Ottoman Christians in their works, no matter how sincere they are, as he heard it himself from the editor of this newspaper which published that conversation, and others.

Islam's role in governance and society

The state of Muslims today and the emergence among them of the call to unify and unite political and religious authority in a single person within all Muslim lands[18]

I can assure Monsieur Hanotaux that this call has no effect in any Muslim land. Had he made any effort to understand their circumstances as they really are he would not have bothered to even allude to this call, let alone base his judgement upon it. Those delusions emerged due to the poor understanding of some Eastern Christians who then reflected them in the minds of Western politicians, and ill will may well have played a role in magnifying such deluded understanding.

I convey the truth authentically without any false veneer or deceptive embellishment. I hope this clarification will convince Monsieur Hanotaux of the good intentions of Muslims in their discourse on religion, and that it will return the editor of the newspaper, which printed their conversation, and others like him, back to their senses, such that they and the people of their lands can be mindful of God and not turn peace into war nor tranquillity into unrest.

18 This was the title under which the article was published in *al-Mu'ayyad*.

I do not deny that there has been a sudden religious urge in recent years in the minds of some Muslims around the world and a divine spirit has passed through the souls of some noble Muslims amongst them and stirred up their zeal to investigate the past conditions of the adherents of this faith, compared to where they are now. There are some of them who share their thoughts when they find a chance to do so and some who spread their views through books or newspapers if they have the means for that. Then, there are imitators of these people who speak without knowledge and utter nonsensical statements. We have nothing to say about these imitators. Rather, we will discuss the goals of those investigators.

Islam did not emerge solely as a spiritual or purely materialistic movement, but rather, as a humane moderate between the two, taking a share from both. Consequently, it conforms to human nature in a manner that nothing else does. Thus, it named itself the religion of human nature and its opponents know it as that until today – it is considered the first school which propelled barbarians up the ladder of civilisation. It is not one of its principles to 'Render unto Caesar what is Caesar's'. Rather, it is its nature to hold Caesar accountable and prevent him from despotism.

This religion came in the manner that we mentioned. It guided the misguided, softened the rigid, refined the coarse, educated the ignorant, awakened the sluggish, inspired the lazy to act, liberated the dependant, reformed the corrupt, and revived dead virtues. Then, it united what was dispersed, mended the breach, rebuilt what had collapsed, wiped out injustice and established justice, renewed the law, and instituted a system for communities that joined it that stood above those of others. As a result, the religion is, for its adherents, Man's perfection, tranquillity at home, and a system for governance. The effects of its blessings are apparent in all their affairs. Knowledge remains integral to it and serves as the authority across all its domains.

If one wanted to say that the faith did not teach them trade, industry, political theory, or day-to-day living, he cannot deny that it made it mandatory for them to work towards that which their individual and societal lives depend upon, and made it mandatory for them to do well in all that. Rulership has also been allowed for them and they are also required to do well in that.

What do you think of a faith whose second caliph, in the city of Yathrib in the Arab lands, said: 'If a lamb on the banks of the Euphrates were to be taken by a wolf, Umar will be asked about it.' Its fourth caliph asked: 'Should I be satisfied with the title "Commander of the Faithful" without partaking in their difficulties or demonstrating resilience when faced with a difficult life?' By that, he meant that he wanted to be equal with the destitute regarding their livelihood, to be an exemplar of kindness for the wealthy, and an example of patience for the destitute.

This is how Islam was an incentive for Muslims, encouraging them to perform great acts. It was a guiding light for them which illuminated their path towards a deeper understanding of circumstances and the rectification of their thoughts. It made their hearts more forgiving and merciful towards others, dealing with them kindly such that the world was content with them as their leaders, and the result of this (i.e. the relationship between Islam and the other) is already known.

After this, is anyone surprised if they see a Muslim who is pleased by what this wise adviser recommends for him and detests that which it disapproves for him? Is it a surprise that the Muslim ridicules anything not aligned with his faith, even if it entails mastery of the earth and the heavens, after the effects that he has witnessed of God's favours in this religion? There is nothing unusual about it – it is an inevitable outcome aligned with God's habit in His creation.

How unfortunate that a Muslim's trust in the religion is all that remains of it. In the Muslim's mind, the religion has been subject to alteration, a shift in its essence, and a change in their understanding of its reality, and its path has vanished from their sight. The saying of Ali, may God honour him, truly applies to him: 'These people have embraced Islam back-to-front like a man who wears a fur back-to-front.'

Currently, I will not investigate the reasons that have led Muslims to where they are now, but I will say, and I fear no reproach for what I say: things have seeped into the religion of the Muslim which are foreign to it and have penetrated his beliefs from sources he does not perceive and which have no connection to its foundation. Rather, they destroy its principles and foundations.

Heretical beliefs and actions have emerged, taking the position of sound doctrine and displacing the Straight Path. Its effects are tangible and its evils have pervaded all spheres.

Whether the tradition of the Prophet which states that 'seeking knowledge is a duty upon every male and female Muslim' is true or not, the Qur'ān affirms its meaning and the actions of the *Salaf* serve to validate its authenticity. Thus, men and women are equally instructed regarding commandments, and possess equal knowledge of the obligatory acts and necessary tenets of the faith. They are both obligated to seek knowledge which will be good for their temporal and eternal lives, and also that which may improve their relations with others, whether related or not, according to the details known in the Book of God and the practices of His Messenger and the works of the pious people who followed him. They should endeavour to enter every realm of knowledge, as much as they are able and as much as time permits.

The Muslim veered off course in the pursuit of knowledge; he was misled to believe that the goal of religious knowledge is to know the outward obligations of ablution, prayer, and fasting. As for the ethical meanings of those acts and the means of making them acceptable to God, such a notion is limited to the minds of a rare few. As for the morality of the faith, spiritual refinement, and the actualisation of noble traits – the real aims of Islamic law and its raison d'être – they are seldom sought after, nor have they become the goal, except for a few individuals scattered throughout the world, lacking the ability to construct a nation and remaining unheard.

As for those who have dedicated themselves to the pursuit of knowledge, making it the cornerstone of their existence, they can be divided into two groups:

The First Group: Those who think of themselves as inheritors and preservers of religious knowledge. These individuals are few in most Islamic lands with only external rituals remaining, often unnoticed by an observer. As for those who keep themselves busy with this in places such as Egypt and Istanbul, all that the intelligent among them can hope for is to look at some specific books which were chosen for them by the passage of time and by poor intuition.[19] They understand such books by way of making

19 ʿAbduh uses the title of *al-Āsitāne* (Ottoman Turkish: 'Threshold') in reference to Istanbul. See Korkut Buğday, *The Routledge Introduction to Literary Ottoman*, trans. Jerold C. Frakes (Abingdon, UK: Routledge, 2009), p. 200.

sure that a certain word provides a certain meaning and, whenever this correspondence takes place, then their mission has been accomplished, whether their mind, faith, and manners are in a good state or not.

They can be compared to people who have inherited a weapon and their only concern is to inspect it. They cannot take their eyes off it but they never extend their hand to use it or remove its rust. As a result, the rust soon spreads and renders the weapon useless. They claim that religion is devoid of any valuable knowledge that goes beyond their current understanding. These people think that they have no business with the masses and that they have no duty to enjoin what is right and forbid what is wrong. In doing so, they have committed an unparalleled error. The misconceptions held by many, or rather, most of them, in understanding the faith are innumerable. It is obvious that this group's attainment of knowledge does not have the slightest effect on reforming the community, as can be seen.

The Second Group: Those whose family prepares them to attain a government position, whether of high or low rank. The individuals in this group, whether many or few, learn the principles of known fields in contemporary sciences and, thereby, each of them attains a position that his father has prepared for him. However, all that is learned is memorised words or stored notions, and the end goal is the mere acquisition of a certificate.

Some of them go to Europe to complete their education, with this being the only aim. If they attain employment, they content themselves with it and limit their efforts to its demands, and those who do not stand waiting at the doors. If the waiting becomes too tiresome or the time for work has passed you will find them in a cafe spending their time and wasting their talents. The righteous among them – which are few – are unconcerned with the state of the masses, whether they are doing well or not. What effect can be seen in the community from these individuals' education? I exempt the anomalies in every region, despite their weakness, and it is hoped their number will increase and the community will benefit from the fruits of their labour.

This is the state of knowledge among men. As for women, a veil has been dropped between them and the obligatory knowledge of their religion and worldly matters, and no one knows when it will be lifted. It does not occur to any of them to study theology or perform religious duties other than fasting. As for their claimed preservation of their chastity, it is only done out of habit and due to the limits set by timidity, or traces of an inherited belief in permissible and impermissible acts. Their minds are full of superstitions and their conversations are mere fancies, other than a few of them whom one could list within a minute.

Yet, both men and women consider themselves to be true Muslims and falsely promise themselves paradise and eternal happiness.

The Muslim is mistaken in his understanding of the concept of *tawakkul* (reliance upon God) and of *qadr* (His foreordainment), so he has inclined towards laziness and inactivity, entrusting his affairs to circumstances which are susceptible to the blowing of the wind. In doing so, he thinks he is pleasing his Lord and fulfilling his religion's aspirations.

The Muslim misunderstands when his religion tells him that Muslims are the best community and that honour and power are tied to their religion for all eternity. He assumes that goodness is tied to the title 'Muslim' and that high status is associated with that word, even if no aspect of its true meaning is actualised, and that God guarantees to support it (i.e. Islam) without any effort from the servant in defending it. If he is afflicted by some problem or faces a calamity he quickly appeals to God's decree and waits for the unseen to intervene, without taking any means to lift the affliction or rising for action to remove the problem he is presented with. In doing so, he contradicts the Qurʾān and the practice of God's prophet.

The Muslim misunderstands the meaning of obedience to those in authority and following their orders, so he entrusts the ruler with the reins of power and entrusts him to act freely in all his affairs. Then, he leaves everything completely to the government and assumes that it can deal with all his affairs through administration and policy without any help from him other than the taxes they impose upon him.

Whoever sees the grief of parents when their children are enlisted in the army, and the efforts they make to free them from that, will judge that what most Muslims understand of the meaning of government does not have any congruence with rationality and will know that their trust in the ruler has reached the level of deification, in that they think he is capable of all things without help from anyone. That trust has transformed into abandonment and desertion in that they have left him and his affairs and do not support him in important matters unless they are compelled to do so.

And who can perform well only if he is forced to undertake something? As a result, the Muslim gradually turns a blind eye to public affairs and his feelings about good and bad affairs weaken unless he is affected directly.

As for the rulers, while they are the most capable of raising the community, they have been afflicted by ignorance regarding the necessity of fulfilling their duties in the same way that most of the masses have. The only meaning they understand of governance is to subjugate people to their whims and to subdue them to the harshness of their authority, as well as to usurp wealth to fulfil their desires. They do not take justice into consideration, nor do they consult the Qur'ān or follow the practice of the Prophet, such that they corrupt the standards of everyone due to their hypocrisy, lying, cheating, oppression, and the qualities that follow that, once they become widespread, become susceptible to facing God's punishment.

All of this has led to many innovations in various schools of theology, opposing methods of action, contradictory views of law, and blind imitation in all of that. Inclinations have diverged, objectives have become divided, and capriciousness has taken the lead between all these competing parties; each of them calls to themselves without looking to the truth and with no fear of falling into falsehood, and his only concern is to triumph over his opponent, and his opponent is the one whom he calls a brother in Islam in a mere display of pretentious speech.

More than that, and this is the biggest innovation facing Muslims in their beliefs, is the innovation of losing hope in themselves and in their faith and thinking that there is no cure for the corruption of the masses and no way to alleviate the adversity that has befallen them. They believe that no day passes them by except that the next one will be worse.

A disease runs its course within them and a sickness has settled in their hearts due to their abandonment of what is decisive in God's book and the practice of His prophet, and their attachment is to unreliable traditions and misunderstandings of the reliable ones. This is a most serious illness annihilating their hearts and minds. Suffice to signify its seriousness is the verse that says: 'Only disbelievers despair of God's mercy.'[20]

20 Qur'ān 12:87.

All these innovations – as well as others which are too numerous to mention – were followed by scant ambition, frail determination, contradictory opinions, cognitive dissonance, and corrupt conduct beginning at home and ending in the community, affecting every stratum and all fields, particularly the field of governance.

As for the blind religious fanaticism that Muslims have been charged with, it only exists in certain Islamic lands in accordance with these misguiding innovations. However, I do not accept that they have gone to extremes in this to even the slightest degree that Christian nations have – Eastern or Western – and history is a truthful witness.

This is what has afflicted the thinking, determination, and actions of Muslims due to their innovations in their faith, their error in its foundations, and their ignorance of its most basic details. Accordingly, God placed people in authority over them who stripped them of the blessings that they were ungrateful for and afflicted them with consequences for their ingratitude that they had no power to repel, unless He sets things right for them out of His grace. God tested them with those who accuse Islam of every flaw, and they only mention it in association with shame, deeming it to be a barrier to civilisation; rather, they consider it the source of their misfortune and the cause of their annihilation.

Consequently, certain discerning Muslims took notice during the middle of the previous century in various regions, such as Persia, India, the Arabian Peninsula, and then Egypt. All of them researched the illness and prescribed suitable medication, according to their understanding. Despite the differences between them, perhaps they will one day meet at the intended goal, God willing.

Their collective objective is to utilise Muslims' trust in their faith to rectify their affairs. It can be said that their goal is to rectify beliefs and eliminate misconceptions in interpreting the texts of the religion until beliefs are safe from heresies. Once achieved, their acts will be free of defects and flaws, their individual affairs will be rectified, their minds will be illuminated by real knowledge – religious and worldly – and their manners will be refined with good qualities. This reform will then spread to the wider community.

If you ever hear of one who promotes studying the faith, this is his aim, or one who encourages religious upbringing, this is his goal, or one who criticises Muslims' corruption, that is his objective.

This is the only straight path for anyone who intends reform among Muslims, no other. To approach them through means of literature or mere philosophy is to ask them to construct an entirely new edifice when they have nothing of its raw material, nor is it easy for them to find those who can put it into practice.

If the religion guarantees the refinement of character, and the rectification of behaviour, and leads people to the gates of happiness, and its adherents already have confidence in it, as we have explained, and it is present among them such that the effort required to restore it is less demanding than establishing something unfamiliar, then why the abandonment of it for something else?

Those who promote a return to the faith, whether in Egypt or elsewhere, do not even consider inciting strife against the Europeans or other neighbouring regions of the Muslims. However, some Christians avoid understanding anything they hear about Islam and create a spectre in their imaginations which they fear and then refer to as Islam, while others assume that if the Muslims were to pay attention to their affairs and return to a correct understanding of their faith, they would gain support through their unity and help themselves to rectify their own affairs, thereby having no need for outsiders who have interfered with their operations. Consequently, this would prevent many Christians from attaining the spoils which they have attained through Muslim negligence. Anyone who believes this has a poor assumption of himself, as he believes himself to be a cheater, a deceiver, and a plunderer. It is also a poor assumption of Muslims, as the people of a nation need one another, no matter how elevated their understanding and how great their efforts. Ultimately, the objective is that the one who gains anything must do so justly, especially if it was initially gained unjustly. Namely, the foreigner who spent nothing but gained everything must return to a sense of balance in his earnings, requiring some effort on his part.

Christians have been working in Muslim polities while they were at the height of their power, and foreigners sought gains within their territories while at their highest state of might.

Yes, this would mean that a Muslim in Egypt can seek the aid of one in Syria, India, Persia, Afghanistan, or elsewhere, as all are afflicted by the same illness – heresies in the faith. Thus, if the medication is successful in one place, then the healed patient will be an example for the sick patient in another. As for striving for unity among Muslims while they are as they are, it is not a consideration for any of them. If one sought this, it would be fitting to send him to the psychiatric hospital.

Some Muslim authorities have spoken extensively on the wisdom of the *Hajj*, saying that it is a link between Muslims from around the world and one of the best ways for them to come to know one another, so they must benefit from it. This is true, but it must be understood correctly, as the aim is for Muslims to remember the communal nature of their faith so that they can support one another in reforming the corrupted elements of their beliefs and the deficiencies in their actions and in repelling famine, oppression, and difficulties they face. This is recognisable to all nations who share a faith, especially among the Europeans.

Muslims today often mention the Ottoman state and Sultan Abdülhamid (r. 1876–1909), pinning their hopes on his ambitions.[21] Many of them promote loyalty to him, a matter of no surprise to anyone, as this polity is the largest Islamic polity today, and its Sultan is the most honoured ruler, and it is hoped that he will lead the Muslims out of their straits. He is the most capable person to rectify their affairs and to support those who call for the rectification of beliefs, the refinement of manners, and a return to the pure roots of the faith.

What about all this vexes Europe, such that they unite to harm the rights of Muslims in the way they did in the past, as Monsieur Hanotaux says?

I still need to address the combining of state and religious authority in one individual. Monsieur Hanotaux states that Europe did not progress until they separated the two, which is correct. However, he does not understand the concept of combining both authorities in one individual for the Muslims.

Muslims never experienced the religious authority which the Pope had among the Christian nations when he would depose kings, excommunicate rulers, and place taxes upon landowners, establishing divine laws.

The Islamic way has affirmed rights for the highest authority – the

21 The reign of Abdülhamid II (d. 1918) witnessed the peak of the *Tanzimat* (Turkish: 'Reorganisation') movement, and he pursued pan-Islamism in response to Western involvement in Ottoman affairs.

caliph or sultan – which are not for the judge, who is the guardian of religious authority. Rather, the sultan is the director of the internal policies of the land and the protector of it by war or diplomacy. The religious scholars do their duties, and he has no rights over them other than patronage and dismissal, and they have no rights over him other than upholding his decrees and removing injustice when possible.

This Ottoman state established civil laws in its lands, legislated a system for rule, and increased the number of rulers and their denominations. It has allowed there to be Christian members in its courts, as well as people from other communities who are under their rule.

Likewise with the government of Egypt. There were both heterogeneous and homogeneous courts established by the order of the ruler. The state of these courts and their laws is known and religion has no place there. The state authority has the final say, as sought by Monsieur Hanotaux, but, despite that, there has been no benefit for reforming the state of Muslims. In fact, it has been the opposite.

If our prior rulers considered themselves religious rulers, they would not have openly carried out oppression and levied excessive taxes or have squandered them in a manner which led to the suppression of Muslim lands and made them lose their most important quality, self-determination.

France calls itself the protector of Catholicism in the East and the British Empire calls itself a Protestant empire. The Tsar of Russia is both king and leader of the Church. Therefore, why is it not allowed for Sultan Abdülhamid to be called the caliph of the Muslims or *amīr al-muʾminīn*?[22]

I do not think that Monsieur Hanotaux has a poor opinion of religious activity in the way that I explained and I think he will be a helper for Muslims by supporting them in French Muslim territories if he finds people who can put this into proper practice. After that, I guarantee him that the welfare of the Muslims will be consistent with the welfare of the French. If Muslims refine their attitude through their faith, they will compete with the French in learning the sciences and attaining understanding, and they will reach their civilisation. With that, harmony between the two will be facilitated, God willing.

22 Commander of the faithful, adopted by numerous Muslim leaders throughout history though rarely invoked by Ottoman sultans.

Ottoman–European relations

Muslims' poor opinion of all European policies, their politicians' lack of trust in all states, Muslims' belief that the welfare of Christian Europe contradicts Islamic welfare, and their lack of trust in the administration of Christian nations, such that they have lost trust in all Christians and do not trust an Ottoman Christian, even if he has been truthful and sincere with them[23]

Monsieur Hanotaux heard about all of that from the editor of the aforementioned newspaper and from some Ottomans in Istanbul and Paris. He then proceeded to prove that Europe is secular and not theocratic.

I am not aware of who those Muslims were that Monsieur Hanotaux described, nor who told him their stories. Were they Indian? They are under the rule of a foreign state and we find, in their speeches and writings, that they obey their rulers and have pinned their hopes on their sense of justice while seeking their rights accordingly.

Were they the Muslims of Russia? Their trust in their government and their government's trust in them is well-known, to the extent that the Russian state has even favoured them over their non-Orthodox Christians. Were they Afghans? The sincerity of their ruler in his cordiality towards the English is more famous than can be stated, but this does not negate his enthusiasm for his own country and his preservation of its welfare.

Were they Persian? Their compliance with Russian rule is known to all.

Were they Moroccan? They are not engaged in anything resembling politics. Moreover, they are heedless of both secular and religious matters. They are occupied with themselves, and they will keep fighting amongst themselves until God alone brings an end to that.

Are they Tunisians? Monsieur Hanotaux has rightly praised them and has affirmed their contentment with French authority merely because of the religious freedom afforded to them.

Perhaps he was only referring to Ottomans as the remainder of his speech indicates and as can be understood from his saying 'and they do not trust an Ottoman Christian', and there are Egyptian and non-Egyptian Ottomans.

---

23 This was the title under which the article was published in *al-Mu'ayyad*.

As for the Egyptians, nothing indicates their lack of trust in Europeans or Christian Ottomans. They work alongside their Coptic citizens in all spheres of government other than the *Sharī'a* courts which are specifically for Muslims. They are in accordance with one another, especially the sincere and pure-intentioned among them; each group has friends and close associates from the other. Their condition is the same as the other Christian denominations, except for those who demonstrate strong fanaticism towards their faith and affect others due to nothing other than blind dogmatism.

The most appropriate witness for this is the editor of the newspaper himself who spoke with Monsieur Hanotaux. Despite his initial opposition to Muslims during the Russo-Turkish War and his questionable conduct after the events of the 'Urābī revolt, the Muslims saw him as a friend and as one who strived for their betterment.[24] He proudly acknowledged this several times in his newspaper, though traces of his negative traits still emerged in his recent conversation. Where can one find this loss of trust in Ottoman Christians in Egypt? Has anyone been expelled from their post simply for being a Christian Ottoman? Has anyone been prevented from being a lawyer, starting a newspaper or a press, or establishing a factory or a trading station based on their status as an Ottoman Christian? Let our friend bring even one witness to support these claims.

As for their position towards Europeans, they make a point of acknowledging justice when perceived in an Englishman and express gratitude if they receive a favour from a European administrator. Moreover, someone seeking assistance against the government will request the appointment of an Englishman to rectify the injustice, as witnessed in many complaints; there were not an insignificant number of complaints made to Lord Cromer, and he is not even an official judge.[25] What could be stronger evidence of trust than this?

24 Named after Aḥmad 'Urābī Pasha al-Miṣrī, an Egyptian nationalist who spearheaded a socio-political initiative channelling the dissatisfaction of educated Egyptians, military personnel, and rural communities towards foreign domination. For details on 'Abduh's involvement with the protest, see the Introduction.

25 Evelyn Baring, 1st Earl of Cromer (d. 1917), was a prominent British statesman and colonial administrator. He served as the British controller-general in Egypt in 1879 and later became the agent and consul-general in Egypt from 1883 to 1907 during the British occupation prompted by the 'Urābī revolt (see above).

Many Egyptians trust the French, and those who have French friends rely on them and pledge their loyalty to them. Monsieur Hanotaux and the editor of this newspaper he spoke with are both aware of that.

French and American teachers in Egypt would often lure Muslim youth into abandoning their faith and adopting Christianity and encourage them to leave Egypt and move to a foreign land, breaking their parents' hearts in the process. Despite that, we still see Muslim parents sending their children to their schools and our Minister of Education, a Muslim, sends his children to a Jesuit school, and the children of many prominent Muslims are in friars' schools. How much more trust can there be than this?

Muslim Egyptians' trust in Europeans increased, especially in business dealings, until the Europeans abused it, seized their opportunity, and usurped many of the possessions of the wealthy. Nonetheless, they still trust them and are excessively compliant with them, imitating them even in matters which contradict their faith and customs. How much more trust is required than this?

Do the intelligent Muslims in Egypt complain of anything more than their blind trust in the Europeans without distinguishing whether they act with sincerity or disloyalty, truthfulness or dishonesty, trust or deception, contentment or greed? This has led to the current state of financial decline and poor conditions.

Is this the loss of trust in Europeans and Ottoman Christians which was meant by the noble editor of the newspaper and his excellency Monsieur Hanotaux?

As for non-Egyptian Ottomans, even if we go as high as the Ottoman sultanate itself, we find the system of the state operated by the work of Christians in the administration and the courts in every land which had Christians. The Christian police commissioners attained the same ends and ranks as the Muslims in relation to their numbers, or even more, and many Christians attained benefits and distinctions which no Muslim did – Christians held positions in the embassies and high-ranking positions of the state.

Sultan Abdülhamid's appeal to the leaders of Christian denominations, his showering them with military medals, privileging some of them with his company, and his graciousness towards them is continually discussed in the newspapers.

The editor of this newspaper who transmitted this conversation is the best example of that. For a significant amount of time, he has openly spoken in a manner that is displeasing to the state, no less than a Muslim, and then it was facilitated for him – a Christian – to be trusted by the noble Sultan to the extent that he was brought into close proximity, accepted in his company, and *amīr al-mu'minīn* listened to his valuable advice which he published in his newspaper almost two months ago, in support of Monsieur Hanotaux. This was followed by several favours and privileges. What is trust if this is what it is like to lose it?

As for the state's foreign policy, the French often complain about the Sultan's goodwill and trust in the German Empire – a Christian empire – and I do not think they complain about his trust in a Muslim state. The state had unshakeable trust in British policy until certain events took place, the most important of which grew out of the weakness of Mr Gladstone's policies which necessarily led to a period of unease in that trust.[26] Today, we see that trust diminishing. There are men in the state who have trust in the sincerity of Russia and would love for state policy to favour them, and they are Muslims.

What I would love for Monsieur Hanotaux to understand is that the policy of the Ottoman state towards European states is not a religious policy. In fact, it was never religious from the day it came into being until today. Rather, it was, in previous days, a state of conquest and, in later days, one of diplomacy and defence. There was no room for religion in its dealings with European states.

The German Emperor came to Syria to celebrate the opening of a church, so the Sultan went to great lengths to celebrate him to an impressive extent that became well-known.

Christian rulers from Europe come to Istanbul and are welcomed with a celebration that they do not find in any Christian region; huge fortunes are spent on such celebrations when Muslims are themselves in need of the funds consumed by these expenditures. Is that not to be courteous with them and earn their affection? Is there anything after such an expression of affection other than trusting the one expressing affection?

26 William Ewart Gladstone (d. 1898) was a four-time prime minister of Great Britain (1868–74, 1880–85, 1886, 1892–94).

It was possible for the Sultan to suffice with official protocol and not exceed that. However, he fulfilled that which went well beyond official protocol. If we accept that the administration of Europe is non-religious in all aspects, then the same is true of Ottoman policy towards Europe and its Muslims follow that.

If one said that the events with the Armenians are still in people's minds and they attribute it to religious fanaticism, it can be stated in response that enmity with a particular denomination is not indicative of a loss of trust with every Christian from that denomination and others.[27] Furthermore, many Armenians serve the state today and have its trust. This shows the unreliability of those who claim that the origin of those events was religious fanaticism, as Christians and others in the Ottoman territories enjoy more prosperous conditions than Muslims, as we can see ourselves.

If the Europeans were fair-minded, they would be able to understand the reasons for this unrest which appeared time after time in that region and they would come to understand that its origin was in Europe and not in Asia.

I have no issue in stating that Christians in Ottoman territories enjoy a type of freedom of education, upbringing, and other types of goodness that Muslims hope to attain. Is this the epitome of a poor opinion of Christians or a lack of trust in them?

It is not befitting for an author like the editor of that newspaper to generalise his report on all Muslims, as that will cause distress to both the Muslims and the Christians. I truly believe that, during his discussion on Muslims, he had certain people in mind whose views he disagreed with and then projected this onto all Muslims and their politicians.

Monsieur Hanotaux should know that all that was said to him, or that was written by some Ottomans, has no correspondent reality other than in the minds of the one who said it or wrote it. Thus, he must not rely upon it in his law-making and he must verify the matter himself if he wishes to discuss it.

As for his claim that Muslims were unhappy with him due to what he

27 This is a reference to a series of brutal acts committed by Ottoman forces against Armenians in the Ottoman Empire from 1894 to 1896. Often termed the 'Hamidian massacres', they are named after Sultan Abdülhamid II, who ruled during this period, to differentiate them from the later Armenian Genocide in 1915.

wrote about Islam, though he often served them, and then he asks: 'How are they towards one who does not serve them?' We will make their perspective on that clear to him to remove his misunderstanding:

If he had been content to speak about politics and investigate the connection between Muslims and his government without attacking two of the most important principles of the faith itself, then not a single person would have held it against him other than someone who wanted to critique his view regarding that which was correct and that which was incorrect. However, he was not content with that. He criticised the doctrine of affirming God's unicity and explained its ill effects on Muslims, then he unsheathed his sword against the doctrine of predestination and explained the negative outcome it has driven them towards. Accordingly, he has affirmed that Muslims will remain in a state of decline for as long as they remain Muslims, which is not an agreeable presumption for any of them.

Had he come to Muslims as they actually are today with their deviation from the principles of their faith, and was content to reprimand them for their negligence in their affairs and their heedlessness about their own welfare, as has been mentioned in the discussion we are having, he would have found the Muslims taking heed of his words and accepting his advice. Regards.

Reflections[28]

These Europeans base their critique of Islam on the poor conditions of Muslims, though they are ignorant about the truth of the matter. The Qur'ān is pure and Islam is pure. Muslims have tarnished it with their disinclination towards everything the Qur'ān contains and their preoccupation with meaningless matters.

28 'Abduh said these words when presented with a criticism of Islam that the Prophet only taught of God's sovereignty and power and that He only required them to dominate other nations.

The Persecution of Knowledge and Civilisation under Christianity *in response to Farah Antun*

In issue number eight of its third year of publication, *al-Jāmi'a* noted – during a discussion about Ibn Rushd's fate – that people hold a range of opinions about the question of whether Christianity demonstrates greater toleration regarding science and philosophy, or if it is Islam which is more accommodating of theorists in these fields.[1] As for those who state that Christianity is more tolerant in these matters than Islam, *al-Jāmi'a* noted that they justify this view by arguing that Voltaire, Diderot, Rousseau, and Renan all said what they said in opposition to religion, yet remained unharmed. Conversely, Ibn Rushd (d. 1198) did no more than affirm and elucidate that which was already established by Aristotle, all whilst preserving his own religious beliefs, and yet was humiliated and spat at. As for those who argue that Islam is more open-minded, they point out that no one was ever burned at the stake for heretical beliefs in Islam, whereas there have been innumerable instances of this under Christianity.

[*Al-Jāmi'a*] then allowed those who hold the first view to have the final say in the matter by stating:

1 This refers to an article in *al-Jāmi'a al-'Uthmāniyya* (The Ottoman Community) written by Farah Antun (d. 1922), one of the first Lebanese Christians to openly argue for secularism and equality regardless of religious affiliation, in which he argued that Christianity is more supportive of science and philosophy than Islam by noting the opposition faced by the twelfth-century Islamic philosopher Ibn Rushd. For more details, see the Introduction. Also see Mark Sedgwick, *Muhammad Abduh: Makers of the Islamic World*, (Oxford: Oneworld, 2010), pp. 88–9.

> Advocates of the first view may respond by asking: must tolerance only be demonstrated within a particular community, or should it also be extended to members of other communities as well? Do [those who argue for Islam's tolerance] not recall the wars and conflicts that took place between different Islamic factions and their rulers based solely on matters of religious belief, which weakened the Islamic community as a whole and caused irreversible schisms therein? Thus, is it possible to refer to the condemnation and execution of a single person as a 'war against humanity', whilst not referring to attacks against entire peoples and communities in similar terms?

The article goes on to state that it will not adjudicate between these two views. However, it did pass two judgements. Firstly, it said:

> Civil and religious authority are closely tied together in Islam by the rule of revelation and, therefore, the general ruler is both governor (i.e. civil authority) and caliph (i.e. religious authority) in one. Consequently, this makes religious toleration harder to come by [in Islam] than it is in Christianity, wherein there took place an unprecedented separation between the two aforementioned fields of authority, which paved the way for the world towards true culture and true civilisation. This took place with a single phrase: 'Render to Caesar the things that are Caesar's and to God the things that are God's.' Thus, in Christianity, the civil authority would be guilty of an appalling crime against humanity if it left any room for the religious authority to put pressure on the private beliefs of individuals, let alone kill them and shed their pure blood across the land. If that were the case, there would not be more toleration in Islam than in Christianity when the latter is unintentionally deficient, even if this unintentional deficiency is more substantial than that of its counterpart (i.e. Islam), because there is no deficiency worse than that of one who has the capacity for proficiency (i.e. Christianity).

Secondly, it stated:

> Until now, science and philosophy have been able to overcome

> Christian suppression. This is why they were each cultivated in the fertile soil of Europe, wherein they brought forth the harvest of modern civilisation. Conversely, they were unable to overcome Islamic suppression, and this provides concrete proof that Christianity is more tolerant [than Islam].

The succinct response

I hasten to briefly demonstrate the falsehood of these two judgements. As for the first point, if the Bible had separated religious and civil authority with a single phrase, the Qur'ān did so unequivocally with two phrases, rather than a single one. God says in the Chapter of the Cow: 'There is no compulsion in religion: true guidance has become distinct from error, so whoever rejects false gods and believes in God has grasped the firmest hand-hold, one that will never break. God is all hearing and all knowing.'[2] And He states in the Chapter of the Cave: 'Now the truth has come from your Lord: let those who wish to believe in it do so, and let those who wish to reject it do so.'[3] As for their second point, I ask *al-Jāmi'a*: Where is the suppression against the Muslim scholars of today? By scholars, I intend those who are equal to the names mentioned by *al-Jāmi'a*, such as Voltaire, Diderot, Rousseau, and their like. And how audacious of *al-Jāmi'a* to state this, whilst it is published in Egypt, an Islamic country whose current condition is clear to see. If it wishes to observe the state of the relationship between Christianity and science today, then it should go to Spain for a short while and judge. It will find hundreds of Muslim students of the sciences in Christian schools, such as those of the Jesuits, Friars, and the Americans – and those are faith schools, especially those of the Jesuits. Now, would I be able to find a single Christian student in an Islamic school even though they allow entry for students of all religious backgrounds? Few students of this kind are found in state schools, as they know that these are secular schools whose curriculums are not faith-based. But is it ever said that a father has oppressed his son by sending him to a Christian school run

2 Qur'ān 2:256.
3 Qur'ān 18:29.

by clergymen? Is this considered a part of Islam's tolerance for science today?!

If it were not for the fact that the scope of this essay was limited to tolerance in regard to science and philosophy, I would have mentioned to the author of *al-Jāmiʿa* that there are two denominations in his country (i.e. Lebanon), thousands in number, each claiming that they have some connection to Islam, whilst believing in that which is incompatible with core Islamic doctrines, including monotheism and the denial of Divine incarnation, nor do they believe in any of its obligatory acts which are known by necessity.[4] This is when the jurists of our community unanimously agree that those two denominations are comprised of apostates and heretics – their slaughtered meat cannot be lawfully consumed and they are not allowed to marry Muslim women – and they (i.e Muslim jurists) only differ regarding whether one who repents from such beliefs will have his repentance accepted, with some scholars stating that it will not be accepted. Yet, they live amongst the Muslims, and have done so for over 900 years, and they continued to live under Muslim rule when it was at the height of its power. Adherents of these denominations entered the Turkish Empire when the French King sought the aid of its King (i.e. Ottoman caliph) whose army was at the gates of Vienna. Thus, those people who were seen by Muslims to have abandoned their faith and adopted beliefs contrary to theirs, whilst engaging in practices contrary to theirs, lived under their rule and could have easily been wiped out by them. And yet, they remain present today and retain bonds of love and friendship with Muslims, and vice versa. So, I ask, has there been any such equivalent amongst Christians?

As I stated earlier, the scope of this essay is limited so I will not diverge from it, and it has led me to articulate my succinct response. Nonetheless, this does not suffice to refute what was alluded to in *al-Jāmiʿa* wherein it rhetorically asked: 'If tolerance must only be demonstrated within a particular community or if it should it also be extended to members of other communities as well,' nor is the validity of its assumption substantiated. A detailed exposition is needed to demonstrate a distinction between the

4 ʿAbduh did not specify which denominations he was referring to here, though his wording seems to indicate a reference to the Yazidis and the Druze.

two religions in terms of their relation to science and philosophy – so that the reader is able to pass his own judgement with understanding – wherein truth is unadulterated by mere conjecture.

The detailed response

I note that *al-Jāmiʿa* raised four issues, and I list them here in the order in which they appeared:

1. Muslims have demonstrated only tolerance towards the free thinkers within their own community, but have not extended this tolerance to members of other religions.
2. There have been adherents of certain Islamic denominations who have been killed for their beliefs.
3. The essence of Islam promotes intolerance towards science and philosophy, whereas Christianity, in its essence, supports Christians in embracing both science and philosophy.
4. Europeans have savoured the fruits of modern civilisation by virtue of Christian religious tolerance.

It is necessary for me to comment upon each and every one of these issues, and I will begin with the second as it has rarely been commented upon.

Denial of inter-fighting between Muslims due to differences of belief

Physical violence between Salafites and Ashʿarites is unheard of throughout Islamic history despite the formidable differences between their doctrines. The same goes for these two Sunnite groups and the Muʿtazilites, despite the considerable divergence between the theology of the Muʿtazilites and that of the Sunnites, both Salafites and Ashʿarites. Likewise, there was never a war between a group of Islamic philosophers and another group. It is true that there were battles known as battles of the Kharijites, just as with the Qarmatians, but these battles were not caused by differences in beliefs. Rather, what ignited them were political views about how to govern the Islamic community, and these groups did not fight with the caliphs in order to promote a particular set of doctrines, but to change the form of governance. As for the conflict between the Umayyads and the Hashemites, it was about the caliphate, and this is more related to politics than theology – rather, it is the core of politics.

It is true that there have been conflicts in recent times that appear to have occurred because of theology, as occurred between the Iranian state and the Ottoman government, or the Ottoman government and the Wahhabites. However, it is easy for one who studies these matters with the slightest bit of consideration to see that these were political conflicts, and this is proved by the enduring amity between these governments today, even though the differences in theology remain between the Ottoman government and Ibn Rashid, the leader of the Wahhabites.

As for the internal conflicts that took place after the establishment of the ʿAbbāsid Caliphate – and which weakened the Muslim community and disunited them – these were conflicts caused by the greediness of the rulers, their corrupted desires and their love of exclusive authority at the expense of all others. The source of all of this was their ignorance about their religion and the loosening of their grip on the rope which tied them to it. The greatest sickness which afflicted the minds and ambitions of the Muslim community only developed because ignorant people were able to seize control of their government. By ignorant, I mean the crude and arrogant people who did not have their ways refined by Islam, and its teachings did not penetrate their hearts. If Allah had granted the Muslims a ruler who knew his religion and governed according to its principles, you would have seen them flourish with the Qurʾān in one hand and that which earlier generations established and later generations discovered in the other hand. That is for their afterlife, and this is for their temporal life – competing with Europeans, nay, overpowering them.

There is no reason for me to discuss rulers here. But that which I must discuss and for which I fear no rebuttal: there is no known war that took place between the Muslims to advance a particular doctrine or because one was abandoned. This is the case, even though what was stated in *al-Jāmiʿa* and compelled us to speak about this topic is not directly related to this point, as the topic of discussion there was about religious tolerance with science and philosophy, not about tolerance for one set of doctrines with another or one religion with another. If it were, then Europe has enough instances of intra-Christian sectarian conflicts and of Christian conflicts with others that it would take the rest of the year's volumes of *al-Jāmi'a,* if we were being brief!

Should I remind *al-Jāmi'a* of the bloodshed that took place in Constantinople between the Orthodox and Catholic churches during the Byzantine period? Should I remind them of the Massacre of St Bartholomew's Day, wherein the Catholics shed the blood of their Protestant brothers, snatched them from their homes, by surprise, and killed them – women, men, and children? Which events, which resulted in the wearing of black mourning attire, should I remind *al-Jāmi'a* of? Is it possible for one to narrate a similar event that happened between Muslim communities due to a difference in doctrines, no matter how great the difference?

Muslims' tolerance of scholars, researchers, and philosophers from all groups

I return to the first of the aforementioned four issues, as there is less to say about it than the third issue. I do not rely upon the works of a Muslim author to point out the consideration that Islam has had for non-Muslim thinkers. Rather, in all that I discuss here, I refer to the books of Christian historians and philosophers. I will note the names of a group of Christians, and others, who attained a level of favour amongst the caliphs and the Muslim masses and aristocrats which no one else attained.

Mr Draper, a historian and one of the great American philosophers, said:

> The early Muslims in the period of the Caliphate did not simply treat the scholars of the Nestorian Christians and the Jews with respect, but they entrusted them with many important duties and promoted them to positions within the state. Even the Caliph Harun al-Rashid placed all of the public schools under the supervision of John Masue, i.e. the well-known Yuhna ibn Maswiya.[5]

5 John William Draper (d. 1882) was an American scientist, philosopher, and historian. His *History of the Conflict between Religion and Science* is considered the origin of the 'conflict thesis', which is the theoretical premise of the intrinsic conflict between science and religion. For more on 'Abduh's interest in Draper's work, see Katsuhata Fuyumi, 'Muhammad 'Abduh and John William Draper', *Annals of Japan Association for Middle East Studies*, 2009, Vol.

He also stated:

> The administration of the schools was delegated, due to the noble vision and open-mindedness of the caliphs, to the Nestorians at times, and to the Jews at other times. It did not matter where a scholar lived or what his religion was, only his intellectual standing was considered. The great 'Abbāsid Caliph al-Ma'mun said: great scholars are the elect from God's creation and the elite from amongst His servants, because they take great care in attaining the benefits of the rational soul, and, by their strength, they rise above the baseness of nature. They are the luminaries and legislators of the world. If it were not for them, the world would descend into ignorance and barbarism.[6]

He also states that 'the Arabs advanced with their armies, including Jewish physicians and Nestorian teachers for their children, and overran the fields of science and philosophy quicker than they had overrun the provinces of the Roman Empire.'[7] Moreover, there is no need for me to mention the schools which were established by the kings and caliphs, and the observatories they commissioned to be built and the books they had gathered in libraries, as this is not relevant to the subject currently under review – it will be mentioned somewhat in that which follows.

Scholars and philosophers who enjoyed the good graces of the caliphs

I mention here some of the scholars who found favour with the caliphs, such as Jurjīs ibn Bukhtīshū' al-Jundīsāburi (d. 768), physician to the Caliph al-Manṣūr (r. 754–775).[8] He was a great philosopher who gained

---

25, No. 1: 165–85, https://doi.org/10.24498/ajames.25.1_165. ʿAbduh alternates between quoting verbatim and paraphrasing Draper's work. Here, ʿAbduh paraphrases. To compare with the original, see John William Draper, *History of the Conflict between Religion and Science*, 10th edn (London: Henry S. King & Co, 1877), p. 105.

6 Paraphrased. To compare with the original, see Draper, *History of the Conflict*, p. 115.

7 Paraphrased. To compare with the original, see Draper, *History of the Conflict*, p. 106.

8 The relative adjective 'al-Jundīsāburi' refers to one who is from the Khuzestan Province in modern-day Iran. See 'Abd al-Karīm al-Sam'āni, *al-Ansāb*, Vol. 3 (Hyderabad: al-'Uthmāniyya), p. 348.

the respect of al-Manṣūr because he had an elderly wife whose lack of attractiveness stemmed from her advanced age, so al-Manṣūr pitied him and sent him three beautiful concubines, but he rejected them, stating: 'My religion does not allow me to marry another woman while my wife is still alive.' Consequently, al-Manṣūr raised his status even beyond that of his ministers. When Jurjīs became sick, al-Manṣūr ordered for him to be carried to a public hospital, whilst he himself walked and asked about his condition. Jurjīs sought the Caliph's permission to return to his own city and be buried with his forefathers. Al-Manṣūr responded by inviting him to convert to Islam so that he may enter heaven, but Jurjīs responded: 'I am content to be with my forefathers in heaven or hell.' Al-Manṣūr laughed and ordered for him to be readied and sent him off with 10,000 dinars – lest we forget, this was al-Manṣūr al-Dawānīqi, who was known for his stinginess. He entrusted whoever was with him to carry him to the cemetery of his forefathers, as he had requested, even if he died along the way. Al-Manṣūr asked him about who could succeed him in his duties, so Jurjīs alluded to 'Īsā ibn Shahlātha, one of his students, so al-Manṣūr appointed him to the position of Jurjīs, but he began to trouble and threaten the priests and patriarchs to acquire what he wanted on account of his standing with the Caliph. The Caliph noticed this and subsequently dismissed him.

Also among those who enjoyed the good graces of al-Manṣūr: the astrologer Naubakht (d. 777) and his son Abū Sahl (d. 923), who were both Persians and followed the Zoroastrian religion. Abū Sahl then had Muslim progeny who were all astrologers who had considerable repute in planetary science.

Among those who attained a high ranking with the Caliph al-Mahdi (r. 775–85) was the Christian astrologer Theophilus ibn Tuma (d. 785) who was of the faith of the Maronites of Lebanon. He wrote a number of great history books and he produced an eloquent Syriac translation of Homer's epic.[9]

Some other specialists who raised their standing with al-Rashīd (r. 786–809) were the physician Bukhtīshu' II (d. 787), his son Jibrīl II (d. 805), and his Syriac Christian son Yuḥannā ibn Māsawaiyh (d. 857), whom al-Rashīd entrusted with the translation of ancient books – in the field of

9 'Abduh does not specify whether this was a translation of *The Iliad* or *The Odyssey*.

medicine and other fields. He served al-Rashīd and the caliphs after him until al-Mutawakkil (r. 847–61), and he would host classes and debates in his house, and there have been no educational gatherings for studying any of the sciences or the arts such as those held in the house of Yuḥannā ibn Māsawaiyh.

In the time of al-Maʾmūn, Yuḥannā ibn al-Biṭrīq, a *mawlā* (client) of al-Maʾmūn, was one of the people whose status was elevated. He was a key translator of works in the fields of medicine and philosophy. Likewise, the rank of Sahl ibn Sābūr was raised, as well as that of his son Sābūr (d. 869), both of whom were Christians, and Sābūr was in charge of Gondishapur's hospital.

Salmawayh ibn Bunān (d. 840) was a Christian physician for al-Muʿtaṣim (r. 833–42). When he died, al-Muʿtaṣim grieved deeply and ordered for him to be buried with incense and candles according to particular Christian customs.

Once, Bukhtīshu' ibn Jibrīl was with al-Mutawakkil, who had him seated next to him. The Caliph wore a silken Roman garment which had a tear in it, and he began to fiddle with it whilst speaking with Bukhtīshu' until the tear widened. Their conversation continued until al-Mutawakkil asked him: 'How do you know when a mentally ill patient requires restraint?' Bukhtīshu' replied: 'When he fiddles with the tear in his garment until it widens, we restrain him,' at which al-Mutawakkil collapsed with laughter.

During the reign of al-Mutawakkil, the Nestorian Christian Ḥunayn ibn 'Isḥāq al-ʿIbādī (d. 873) achieved fame, and he remains one of the most famous translators of the works of Aristotle and other philosophers. Al-Mutawakkil examined his integrity and he demonstrated an unbreakable will, so he allotted him extensive land. Ḥunayn was known for his eloquence and excellent translation in the time of al-Ma'mūn when he was a young man, so he was regularly assigned works to translate and would receive the weight of his translated works in gold. There was a grudge between Ḥunayn and al-Ṭayfūri which led to the bishops being beseeched to ban Ḥunayn from the Church, and Ḥunayn subsequently died of grief due to the persecution he faced from the people of his own community, despite his honourable and elevated status with the Caliph – al-Ṭayfūri was also a favourite of the caliphs.

Another person who attained high standing with the caliphs, as well as the aristocracy and the masses during his lifetime – during the reign of al-Rāḍī – was the Nestorian logician Abū Bishr Mattā ibn Yūnus (d. 940). He was an expert in the rational sciences, and Abū Naṣr al-Fārābī (d. 950) was a student of his as he was the head of the Baghdad school of Aristotelian philosophers. He was born in Dayr Qunna, raised in the school of Marmary, and studied with the two Jacobite ascetics, Rafael and Benjamin.

Another of the favourites of the caliphs and a philosopher of the Islamic polity was Qusṭā ibn Lūqā al-Baʿlabakkī (d. 920). He was a Christian who the caliphs summoned to Baghdad to work as a translator. Then there was the logician Yaḥya ibn ʿAdī ibn Ḥamīd ibn Zakarīyā (d. 974) who was the chief authority in the philosophical sciences of his day and he had been a pupil of both Mattā ibn Yūnus and Abū Naṣr al-Fārābī.

There was also the philosopher Abū al-Faraj ibn al-Ṭayyib (d. 1044) who is said to have held the office of patriarchal secretary in Baghdad. He used to lecture on medicine in the al-'Adudi Hospital, and he was a contemporary of Ibn Sīnā, who praised his knowledge of medicine, though not his knowledge of philosophy, which he critiqued.

Someone else who had a prestigious position with the caliphs, aristocracy, and the masses was the Sabaean Thābit ibn Qurra al-Ḥarrānī (d. 901), of the widely recognised Sabaeans. He was raised in the house of the famous astrologer Muḥammad ibn Mūsa ibn Shākir and he reached a level of expertise in the philosophical sciences that no other has replicated. He wrote a number of treatises in logic, medicine, and mathematics, and the caliph al-Muʿtaṣim would favour him over his own viziers.

Thābit was born in the year 211 of the Islamic calendar in Ḥarrān, and his sons Ibrāhīm ibn Thābit ibn Qurra and Sinān ibn Thābit ibn Qurra followed their father's footsteps. Among his grandchildren was Abū al-Ḥasan Thābit ibn Qurra. Thābit, Ibrāhīm, and Sinān were all Sabaeans, yet they rose to the ranks that you now know, and a number of Muslim poets praised them even though they were Sabaeans.

How many more philosophers and scholars from various religions who lived in the early period of Islam and for whom no effort was spared in affording the utmost respect and patronage should I list for *al-Jāmiʿa*? Do you want me to add to the names of the Muslim philosophers who attained the utmost echelons of prestige among the caliphs and kings? Do I need to mention the philosopher of Islam Abū Yūsuf al-Kindī (d. 870), who was of Basran origin, and whose father Isḥāq was a commander over Kufa under al-Mahdī and al-Rashīd and a descendant of al-Ash'ath ibn Qays, one of the companions of the Prophet? He was a scholar of medicine, philosophy, nature, mathematics, and music theory. Furthermore, he worked as a translator, as did others, and he translated many books of philosophy and included elucidating explanations of key concepts. He held an esteemed rank with al-Ma'mūn, al-Mu'taṣim, and his son Aḥmad. Do I also need to mention the sons of Mūsa ibn Shākir – Muḥammad, Aḥmad, and al-Ḥasan – who all worked in the fields of astronomy and astrology and the station they had with the caliphs and rulers? Should I mention Ibn Sīnā (d. 1037) and the high esteem he was held in by his people and his appointment as vizier during the reign of Shams al-Dawla (r. 997–1021)? Or al-Fārābī and his station with Sayf al-Dawla (d. 945–67) and Ibn Ḥamdān?

There is no doubt that Abū al-'Alā' al-Ma'arrī (d. 1057) is the type of man whose biography *al-Jāmi'a* would be interested in publishing. He made statements that even Voltaire and Rousseau never made, and yet he died naturally in his bed and his gravesite is still visited to this day.

I believe it will be easier now, after what we have recounted here, for the readers of *al-Jāmi'a* to know that Islam used to welcome people of all communities with the same criteria – the respect scholars have for their areas of expertise. However, it is easy for me to find an excuse for *al-Jāmi'a* as to why it wrote what it wrote, believing that it had in mind certain cases that were said to be motivated by religious fanaticism, but in reality had nothing to do with religion. Rather, they were motivated either by foolish politics, or blind ignorance, or the appeasing of some feeble-minded individuals.

I will not prolong this section any further for fear of monotony, and I will now move on to the third issue: a comparison of the essence of the two religions. This is more important than that which has preceded it and that which will follow.

The Essence of Christianity

Introduction

Al-Jāmi'a assumed that Christianity separated religious authority and civil authority, and, as such, that it is tolerant by its very nature. As for Islam, the presence of a ruler – king or caliph – is a religious fundamental and that makes it difficult, in *al-Jāmi'a's* opinion, to be tolerant.

However, this does not suffice to explain the nature of the two religions and their readiness for tolerance with science and philosophy or any belief system that contradicts them. Rather, it is essential to explain the foundations of each religion and its most important principles, which all of its subsidiary points are based upon and which produce its real effects.

Upon examining any religion, to judge in its favour or against it in any particular issue, it is necessary to examine it in its purest form, away from any of the customs of its adherents or their innovations, which may be imported from other religions. So, if one wants to take any speech or action that elucidates some of the fundamental tenets of the religion as evidence for following it, then one should focus on the speech or action of those closest to the time of its origins and of those who received it in its simplest form from the one who preached the religion in the very beginning.

I will summarise my presentation of the first principles which appear in the canonical gospels as they are with Christians now, and which appear in the words of their early fathers, then I will demonstrate what this has led them to by virtue of the essence of their religion.

The first principle of Christianity: miracles

The first principle upon which the Christian religion is based and which serves as its strongest pillar is the belief in miracles. When you read the gospels, you will not find any evidence for the truthfulness of Christ except the miracles which he performed, and their number in the Gospels is too many to enumerate.

Subsequently, those miracles then became the means of proving the authenticity of the religion for those who came after him, as was the case for the disciples, as can be seen in the tenth chapter of the Gospel of Matthew. As such, you will find that of everything that the forefathers of this religion said, miracles serve as the most compelling evidence for the veracity of their beliefs. Of course, a miracle is that which takes place in contradiction to the laws of nature. So, if performing miracles becomes possible for anyone who reaches a high standing within the religion, then no normative laws are truly present, as such, in the Christian tradition.

The Bible goes beyond this by stating that faith, even if it be the size of a mustard seed, is enough to change the laws of nature. In the seventeenth chapter of the Gospel of Matthew it states: 'Verily I say unto you, If ye have faith as a grain of mustard seed, ye shall say unto this mountain "Remove hence to yonder place," and it shall remove; and nothing shall be impossible unto you.'[1] And in the eleventh chapter of Mark: 'For verily I say unto you, That whosoever shall say unto this mountain, "Be thou removed, and be thou cast into the sea," and shall not doubt in his heart, but shall believe that those things which he saith shall come to pass; he shall have whatsoever he saith. Therefore, I say unto you, What things soever ye desire, when ye pray, believe that ye receive them, and ye shall have them.'[2]

However, every investigation which leads to the conclusion that nature has established laws, and that conditions, causes, or preventors all adhere to laws of causes and effects, or that which is impossible so long as they are present, is contradictory to this principle throughout history. Certainly, every subfield of cosmology requires this investigation, which means that science by nature is opposed to this foundational principle. Anyone who believes in this principle does not need to investigate causes and effects, because his belief that something will happen and his will for it to happen

1 King James Bible, Matthew 17:20
2 King James Bible, Mark 11: 23–4.

are enough to actualise it. Thus, he has no need for science when it opposes what he believes. How difficult must it be for a religion like that to tolerate science!

The second principle of Christianity: the authority of the priests

This principle is followed by another, which is the religious authority granted to the priests regarding their beliefs and the cognitive limits of the masses. This authority was granted by the verse which appears in Matthew 16:19, wherein it states: 'And I will give unto thee the keys of the kingdom of heaven: and whatsoever thou shalt bind on earth shall be bound in heaven: and whatsoever thou shalt loose on earth shall be loosed in heaven.' Also, in Matthew 18:18: 'Verily I say unto you, Whatsoever ye shall bind on earth shall be bound in heaven: and whatsoever ye shall loose on earth shall be loosed in heaven.'

So, if the priestly authority declares that someone is not a Christian, he will be deemed as such, and if he declares that someone is a Christian, he will attain salvation because of it. So, the believer is not free in his belief; he cannot believe that which his rationality has guided him to. Rather, the eyes of his heart are tied to that which is upon the lips of his leader. Therefore, if his inner self is driven to investigate, the one who holds that authority can restrain him from doing so. Even if some Christians today oppose this principle, it has been a principle of Christianity for fifteen continuous centuries.

The third principle of Christianity: asceticism

After these two principles comes the third, which is to abandon worldly pursuits and to focus solely on the next life. You will find this principle throughout the Gospels and in Acts of the Apostles; whatever you read of the early scriptures, you will find it. You will find direct commands to turn towards the kingdom of heaven and to abandon worldly life in the sixth, tenth, and nineteenth chapters of the Gospel of Matthew. From the sixth: 'Ye cannot serve God and mammon. Therefore I say unto you, Take no thought for your life, what ye shall eat, or what ye shall drink; nor yet for your body, what ye shall put on. Is not the life more than meat, and the body than raiment?'[3] Also: 'But seek ye first the kingdom of God, and his righteousness; and all these things shall be added unto you.'[4] And I will also quote: 'And again I say unto you, It is easier for a camel to go through the eye of a needle, than for a rich man to enter into the kingdom of God.'[5] In the tenth: 'Provide neither gold, nor silver, nor brass in your purses. Nor scrip for your journey, neither two coats, neither shoes, nor yet staves …'[6]

As encouragement for monasticism and celibacy – and, consequently, the denial of progeny – it says: 'and there be eunuchs, which have made themselves eunuchs for the kingdom of heaven's sake. He that is able to receive it, let him receive it.'[7]

Entry into the kingdom of heaven is dependent upon faith that pays no heed to worldly realities. Therefore, what will one who believes in this principle attain by studying any branch of the sciences, when scientific inquiry has nothing to do with the hereafter and worldly pleasure is forbidden for him? There is no doubt that his sole concern will be prayer and a dedication to worship with all his heart without concern for anything else, and studying the universe is not a form of worship according to him, because worship in the Gospels is simply faith and prayer.

The fourth principle of Christianity: belief in the incomprehensible

After these principles comes the fourth, and it is the foundation of all the others according to most Christians – neither Catholic, Orthodox, nor Protestant differ about it – and it is that faith is a gift that has nothing to do with reason. There are matters of faith that transcend rationality, meaning that they contradict principles of rationality, and they are, despite that, things which one must have faith in. Saint Anselm said: 'You must first believe in that which enters into your heart without looking into it, then try to understand what you have believed in, as faith – which is the only mean for attaining salvation – does not require rational investigation, and

3 King James Bible, Matthew 6: 24–5.
4 King James Bible, Matthew 6:33.
5 King James Bible, Matthew 19:24.
6 King James Bible, Matthew 10:10.
7 King James Bible, Matthew 19:12.

creation and all that it contains does not concern the believer such that he needs to ponder it deeply.'[8] His saying 'then try to understand what you have believed in' makes it a supererogatory act to appeal to the human inclination that naturally seeks to understand what it believes in, but mere faith suffices in the end. Then, woe to anyone who seeks understanding if his efforts to understand lead him to something which contradicts his faith, as if the real meaning of 'understanding' is for the believer to create something within himself which allows him to maintain faith in the incomprehensible.

The fifth principle of Christianity: that the holy scriptures contain everything which mankind needs to know for this life and the next

Added to the four principles is the fifth, which is that the books which make up the Old Testament and the New Testament encompass all knowledge that humankind needs to know, whether it be about religious beliefs or spiritual manners and physical acts, which lead to the attainment of bliss in the kingdom of God, or to do with secular sciences, which are comprehensible by the human mind. Tertullian, the best person to have described Christian doctrine at the end of the third century before many heresies were introduced, said: 'Christian doctrine was established upon the divine scriptures, and the proof of the soundness of these scriptures is their antiquity, for they are older than the book of Homer, and older than any known trace of the Romans or of the establishment of their polity itself, and time supports the truth, let alone that the prophecies contained in those scriptures materialised.' He then said: 'The basis for all knowledge is the Bible and the practices of the Church. God's teachings extend beyond revelation which only serves as guidance towards the religion. Rather, he teaches us with revelation every time he wants us to know Him, and the Bible contains the predetermined measure of knowledge which has been calculated for humankind to attain.' Thus, everything which is in the scriptures pertaining to descriptions of the heavens and the earth and the history of peoples must be accepted whether it contradicts reason or defies

8 'Abduh seems to be paraphrasing from Anselm's *Proslogion.*

sensory perception. People must first believe in it, and then strive after that to understand it whilst accepting it.

Some of their great thinkers have asserted: 'It is possible to learn the science of mineralogy in its entirety from the Bible.'

The sixth principle of Christianity: demarcating between Christians and others – including those with similar beliefs

All of those principles make up the sixth principle – which I consider to be the final one – and that principle is the one which is in the tenth chapter of the Book of Matthew: 'Think not that I am come to send peace on earth: I came not to send peace, but a sword. For I am come to set a man at variance against his father, and the daughter against her mother, and the daughter in law against her mother in law. And a man's foes shall be they of his own household.'[9]

It has been stated in a number of places within the Gospel that the slightest deficiency in loving the Messiah or in obeying everything which he commanded are causes of destruction, even though it has been mentioned many times that faith alone is enough in the end. This is despite the sense of severity which is in the verse: 'Think not that I am come to send peace on earth …' It is the impact of this that remained in the psyches of the first believers in the religion of the Messiah, and it effaced the effects that one must have experienced from the other teachings.

The results and effects of these principles

On this basis, the early Christians shunned the preoccupations of this temporal world and averted people from its study as a way of demonstrating the sufficiency of the faith and of worship over all other things; they restricted people's natural inclinations except those calling to faith and worship, and the means of calling are likewise faith and worship. If certain minds incline towards knowing something about the world, they place the Old Testament in front of them, thereby confining all knowledge to its contents as a means of relying solely on revelation over all other exercises

9 King James Bible, Matthew 10: 34–6.

of the mind apart from understanding its pronouncements. Furthermore, not everyone is qualified to understand it; rather, they take its understanding from the heads of the Church for fear of deviation in their sound faith – with the exception of Protestants who are of the view that exegesis is permissible even by those outside of the Church. Indeed, using the sword and separating families and loved ones has come as a way of protecting all of that. So if an incorrect thought occurs to someone, which could cause any opposition to established matters of faith, that thought must be forcibly preempted, and there is no room for clemency or mercy for the one who thought it, just as the Messiah taught by his own actions according to what is found in the Gospel, as it was said to him: 'Then one said unto him, Behold, thy mother and thy brethren stand without, desiring to speak with thee. But he answered and said unto him that told him, Who is my mother? And who are my brethren? And he stretched forth his hand toward his disciples, and said, Behold my mother and my brethren!'[10] Similar to this can be found which also necessitates separating one who believes in the Christian religion and one who causes any doubt in his belief. It is clear that something starts as a seed, then a plant, and then a tree, so look at what became of these foundational matters by the nature of how things grow and develop.

It is an established fact for Christians that safety is the absence of thought and is instead blind faith, and they have accordingly established the principle that 'ignorance is the basis of piety'. Many religious adherents, Christians and Muslims, still go by this principle as if it is a blessing that they have inherited from past generations, so they restrict education to the monasteries, and the Church prevented the dissemination of education amongst lay people except for that which can be used as a call to piety and establishing outward demonstrations of faith. Other than the priests, the remaining adherents of the faith remained ignorant, even in matters of religion and its realities.

Such was the case, that when Halley's Comet appeared in 1672, the people of Europe were unsettled and sought refuge with the Pope who responded to their call and had it expelled from the sky, so they believed it vanished out of fear of his curse and did not return for another seventy-five years.

10 King James Bible, Matthew 12: 47–9.

It is not allowed for anyone to put forth an opinion which contradicts that which is clearly stated in the Bible, and when Pelagius (d. 418) put forth his view that death predated Adam, that is, that animals used to die even before Adam sinned by eating from the tree, it caused outrage and the controversy ended with the Emperor's edict that anyone who believed in it was to be killed. A historian reported: 'This is how it became a crime against the King to believe that living things used to die before the time of Adam.'

The books of the Ptolemaic period in Alexandria were burned during the reign of Julius Caesar, then Theophilus the Patriarch of Alexandria used the most insignificant reason to launch an insurrection in the city, by destroying what remained of the library of Alexandria, by burning and by simply dispersing it. The historian Orosius (d. 418) said that he saw the shelves of the library empty almost twenty years after Theophilus received the imperial edict to destroy them.

Then, after Theophilus came his nephew Cyril, who was an eloquent orator who had influence over people due to his rhetoric. There was a young woman in Alexandria named Hypatia, a mathematician who was also an astronomer and a philosopher and whom many specialists in mathematics would call upon. All of her gatherings would include some philosophical investigation, especially about the following three matters: Who am I? Where am I going? What can I know? Saint Cyril could not tolerate this, even though the young woman was not a Christian but instead followed the religion of her Egyptian forefathers, so he began inciting the people against her until they ambushed her when she was on the way to one of her study sessions, stripped her naked, and took her to the church undressed, where they killed her. They then mutilated her body, skinned her, and threw whatever remained into a fire. The historian who narrated this story said: 'Cyril was not asked about what he did to Hypatia, and the Roman government did not look into the matter – perhaps this was when the principle was first established that "the ends justify the means".'

There is no religious doctrine that has appeared in Christianity which a group wanted to establish and another group opposed except that blood was spilled over it. If we look back through history, we can imagine the land of Egypt dyed red with the blood of Christians from two different groups when it was desired to establish the worship of the Virgin Mary and to ascribe a mother to God. That was the nature of the religion: that the one who does not follow the Messiah perishes, and the one who perishes does not deserve life. Have you not read the fifth chapter of Acts about the story of the man who sold everything that he had and gave some of the money to Peter and saved the rest for himself, keeping it from him? When Peter found out the truth, he rebuked the man and miraculously caused him to die. Then, when his wife came, and she had known about what her husband had kept hidden and did not stop him, Peter rebuked her and informed her of her husband's death, and she also then died. So, if God would take life as a punishment for one having embezzled some of his own wealth and not gifting it to the Apostles, then how about the life of one who goes against God and resists them in what they believe?

Pope Innocent III (r. 1198–1216),when speaking of the seizure of those who had opposed Catholic doctrine, stated: 'It is not allowed to leave anything for the children of the infidels except their lives, and allowing them to live is a favour and an act of beneficence.' And so, punishment was not limited to the infidels but also extended to their children, and allowing them to live was an act of beneficence towards them as they did not deserve to live once their parents disbelieved.

Christianity's opposition to science

I do not find any mention of science and philosophy throughout history once Christianity attained power during the reign of Constantine and after, except during the religious conflicts that only ended through the intervention of the authority of the kings at times, at others by calling for Christian councils, and thirdly with the shedding of blood, until the light of science faded and mere religion was all that remained. Furthermore, every mention relates to Christianity and other religious communities who lived nearby, by way of forcing the followers of those religions to convert to Christianity, and what took place between the kings of Europe with the mutual shedding of blood motivated by the Church leaders, and that matter is known to anyone well-read in history, and is not the subject of our discussion here.

But I see a semi-conflict between science and religion appear in Europe after the emergence of Islam, and the establishment of its rule in the Iberian Peninsula, and the contact between the Europeans and the Muslims during the Crusades.

Thousands of crusaders returned to their countries and told their people things which contradicted that which had been propagated by the heads of the Church: that the Muslims were pagans who had taken over the Holy Land, removed monotheism from it, erased any purity and virtue from it, and that they were feral beasts and predatory animals. But when the crusaders returned home, they told their people that their enemies were people of religion, monotheism, and honour, and they were honest and virtuous.

Then the Caliph al-Ḥakam II (r. 961–76) made al-Andalus into a paradise, as stated by the American philosopher, and the Jews and Christians came together in that land under the shade of security and freedom.[11] Peter the Venerable (d. 1156) said he 'found learned men even from Britain pursuing astronomy. All learned men, no matter from what country they came, or what their religious views, were welcomed. The Khalif [sic] had in his palace a manufactory of books, and copyists, binders, illuminators …'[12]

Then knowledge of paper production, which the Arabs invented, was spread and the press was invented, and it became easy for people to spread their views after their thoughts were awakened by knowledge transmitted to them from the bearers of science, originating from scholars of al-Andalus and those who conveyed it from surrounding areas. Then, some of that which had been called by the Europeans 'the philosophy of Ibn Rushd' also reached them, and, thereafter, Christianity took notice and began to oppose anything which people stated with their tongues or heard with their ears which contradicted the Biblical scriptures and the traditions of the Church.

Romnis said: 'The rainbow is not a bow in the hand of God to take revenge on his slaves when he wishes to do so, rather it is a reflection of sunlight in drops of water.' Consequently, he was summoned to Rome where he was imprisoned until he died, then his corpse and his books were put on trial and the decree was given for his body and books to be thrown into a fire. It has been said about the reason for this decree: 'He wanted to reconcile between the Churches of Rome and England, and which sin

11 The American philosopher here is again a reference to Draper.

12 The original in Arabic here is a direct translation by ʿAbduh of Draper, see *History of the Conflict*, p. 142.

could be greater than this reconciliation? It is undoubtedly far greater than stating that the rainbow reflects sunlight in drops of water.'[13]

The surveillance of publications and the Inquisition

Publications began to be inspected, and every author and every printer was obligated to present his publication, or that which he wished to publish, to the priest or the council which had been designated for inspection, and decrees of excommunication were issued against those who published anything which had not been presented, or which had been published without the permission of the inspector. The inspector would be advised to read closely so that nothing would be published that included any insinuation that went against the doctrine of the Catholic Church, and heavy fines were placed upon the owners of the publishing houses and they were excommunicated.

The Inquisition to oppose science and philosophy was established when it was feared that the two fields of study would gain prominence due to the students of Ibn Rushd, and the students of his students, particularly in the south of France and Italy. This strange Inquisition was established by the order of the monk Tomás de Torquemada (d. 1498).

The Inquisition did its duty to the utmost, for during a period of eighteen years – from 1481 to 1499 – it sentenced 10,220 people to burning at the stake, and so they were burnt, and for 6,860 people to be hanged after being pilloried, and so they were pilloried and hanged, and for 97,023 people to face various other punishments, and they were all implemented; then every Hebrew Bible was burnt.

What were the methods of investigation used by this Inquisition? One method was for them to imprison the accused and enact various forms of torture with a range of torture devices until the accused confessed to whatever he was accused of, and then they would issue a decree against him and carry it out.

The Lateran council decided in 1502 to condemn anyone who looked to the philosophy of Ibn Rushd, and the Dominican order considered cursing Ibn Rushd and anyone who looked to his philosophy as form of art or

---

13 We were unable to locate a source for this quote.

worship, but that did not prevent rulers and students of all classes from searching for means to attain any of his books or to enrich their intellects with some of his thoughts.

The Inquisition redoubled its efforts to find those criminals, from students of knowledge and those who sought to attain it, and linked to this was the uncovering of heresies and offering judgements against them no matter how well they were hidden: in cities, houses, cellars, tunnels, storerooms, kitchens, caverns, forests, or fields. And this duty was carried out with a joy and giddiness that were felt by those who were protective of their faith, acting upon the scriptural words: 'I came not to send peace, but a sword.'[14]

Monks were apprehended from their hermitages, clergymen from their churches, nobility from their palaces, traders from amongst their goods, craftsmen from their factories, the laity from their homes and fields, and wherever else they were found, and they were stood in front of the Inquisition and judgements would be passed against them the day they were accused.

The Lateran council decided that one of the means of discovering the masses' ideas was mandatory confession, in accordance with Catholic doctrine, in front of a priest in the church.

A daughter, or a wife, or a sister would go for confession with a priest on Sunday, and she would be asked about the beliefs of her father, or husband, or brother, what he would unexpectedly say at home, what he would do whilst among his family, and if the priest felt any suspicion about his seeking secular knowledge, he would bring his case to the Inquisition and the man would be bombarded with accusations. When asked for a witness to support the accusation, there would be no answer. Instead, the family member would themselves be tortured until the accused confessed.

This sacred Inquisition struck fear in the hearts of the people of Europe. When the luminosity of intellectual reflection illuminated one's mind, and he looked around or glanced behind him, it seemed as though the messenger of misfortune was trailing him and that chains and shackles would reach his neck and hands more quickly than the scholarly thought could

14 King James Bible, Matthew 10:34.

manifest. As was stated at that time: 'It is almost impossible for a person to be Christian and die a natural death.'[15]

This Inquisition ruled, from the day of its establishment from the year 1481 until 1808, against 340,000 people, of which almost 200,000 were burned alive.

Christian persecution of Muslims, Jews, and scholars in general

When Ibn Rushd was the fountainhead from which the water of knowledge and freedom gushed out in Europe, as the clergymen claim, he taught many Jews who were then accused of spreading his thoughts and ideas. As he was a Muslim, the Church's wrath descended upon the Jews and Muslims together. Thereafter, it was decreed on 30 March 1492 that any Jew who did not accept baptism, no matter how old or what state he was in, would be obligated to leave Spain before the month of July. If any of them returned to that country thereafter, they would face punishment of death. Prior to leaving, it was allowed for them to sell their movable and immovable assets on the condition that they did not take any gold or silver in exchange but would only accept offers of goods and bills of exchange. And who would pay for something today when he would be able to obtain it after three months for free?! An order was issued by Torquemada that no citizen of Spain offer them any support. Along these lines the Jews left – leaving all that they owned – with their lives, although there was no escape for many of them, as hunger and the difficulties of travel, along with poverty and lack of provisions, killed many of them.

In February of the year 1502, an order was published to expel the enemies of God, the Moors, from Seville and its surroundings. Those of them who did not accept baptism would leave the country of Spain before the month of April – and it was allowed for them to sell what they owned according to the same condition that was set for the Jews. But another condition was set for the Muslims, which was that they should not leave on a road that led to Muslim lands, and the penalty for whoever violated that was death. These poor people were all expelled, either facing death as

15 ʿAbduh attributes this quote to a specific figure, Bāghliyādīs. Despite our persistent attempt to identify this figure, we failed to find any information.

punishment upon returning, or death meeting them along the way due to weariness along with nakedness and hunger.

Would the reader not be astonished if he saw that Bruno was burned alive after a long imprisonment in the year 1600 because he proclaimed the beliefs of the Sufis in regard to the unity of existence, and simply said: 'This world contains many worlds? All praise is to Allah the Lord of all worlds.'? [16]

The notion of Earth's roundness emerged – and that is a fact that the Muslims had already known since the early 'Abbāsid caliphate, and it did not stir a single leaf in the forest – and yet it caused severe turmoil in the Christian world, and the incidents that occurred as a result of this are beyond the scope of this essay.

Does the reader believe that what Christopher Columbus wanted, by exploring in the Atlantic Ocean so that he might discover new land, was a matter of concern to the Church, and that the School of Salamanca ruled that it was contrary to the principles of their faith? Then, it was reconsidered and reviewed in accordance with the sayings of the Church Fathers, such as Chrysostom, Auine, Jerome, Gregory, Basil, Ambrose, and with the Acts of the Apostles, the Gospels, the Prophecies, the Psalms, and the Pentateuch, and this review did not lead to anything, but some rulers helped him to achieve what he wanted regardless of the Church, as is known? Christopher Colombus said: 'This noble endeavour was inspired by the books of Ibn Rushd.'[17] From this, do you understand why the Church was so agitated?

Principle of authority for clergymen over the masses

How strongly has the Church adhered to the hallowed principle: 'Authority is for the priests and obedience is for the masses.' Any opinion which

16 Giordano Bruno (d. 1600) was an Italian philosopher, astronomer, and mathematician. While studying in Naples, he was impressed by the lectures of G.V. de Colle, who was known for his tendencies toward Averroism – i.e. the thought of a number of Western Christian philosophers who drew their inspiration from the interpretation of Aristotle put forward by Ibn Rushd.

17 We were unable to locate a source for this quote.

does not emanate from that religious source – that is, whatsoever ye shall bind on earth shall be bound in heaven: and whatsoever ye shall loose on earth shall be loosed in heaven – then it is fallacious and must be opposed by any means possible. This is why there was a judgement against Galileo, who proposed that celestial mechanics run according to the system known to astronomers today.

Church opposition to hypodermic injections

Do you know about the resistance to administering hypodermic injections? This medical method was discovered by Muslims in Ottoman Istanbul, then a woman named Mary Montagu conveyed it to Europe in the year 1721, so the clergymen became enraged and opposed its use. The help of the King of England was sought in order to support its use, and this intensity of opposition returned when the method for smallpox vaccination was discovered.

Opposition to painless labour

What kind of opposition was not encountered by the discovery of anaesthetising women so that they would not feel the throes of childbirth? An American discovery which the priests thought would rid women of that curse or punishment that had been prescribed for them in the Book of Genesis: 'Unto the woman he said, I will greatly multiply thy sorrow and thy conception; in sorrow thou shalt bring forth children.'[18]

Opposition to civil authority and freedom of belief

The Pope issued a decree in the year 1864 which included an execration of anyone who said that the Church may submit to a civil authority, or allowed for one to interpret anything from the Bible in a manner that contradicted what the Church says, or believe that one was free to choose what he believed and would be judged according to it by his Lord. In a decree by him in the year 1868: 'Believers must sacrifice their lives and wealth

18 King James Bible, Genesis 3:16.

for the authority of the Church and they must relinquish their thoughts and opinions for it, and Rome invited the Orthodox and Protestant churches to submit to the Roman Church in this manner.'[19]

In the year 1871, there was a conflict between the Prussian government and the Pope about the dismissal of a professor from one of the colleges who had an opinion which did not please the Catholics, so the Pope excommunicated him and asked the government to dismiss him. This was a political dilemma, although Otto von Bismarck's (d. 1898) determination helped the civil authority over Church authority in the nineteenth century, so the professor remained, and education was placed under the authority of the civil government.

Opposition to scientific associations and books

I will not mention the scientific associations which were abolished, and the conferences which were suspended. They contained nothing except guidance for mankind on things which benefitted them, and the enlightening of their vision by unveiling that which was hidden from them of the secrets of the universe via speculative inquiry with rational methods and without consulting the godly ruler – that is, the Church – but I will mention one thing: Cardinal Cisneros (d. 1517) burned 8,000 books in Granada with writings containing many translation of works relied upon by European scientists of that era.

Protestantism and Reform

One may say: Everything you have mentioned relates to the actions of the Roman Catholic Church, but Christianity has had a number of reformers, and they have influenced hearts and minds, and after the era in which reform emerged and there was a return to the first principles of the religion, the dawn of knowledge broke in the West and filled the land with tolerance for science, and that can only be in accordance with the essence of religion.

I will not mention anything in response to the above except that the

19 He is probably referring to the papal statement contained in the third chapter of the First Vatican Council. See: https://www.papalencyclicals.net/councils/ecum20.htm

Protestants themselves have mentioned in the history of Reform: capital punishment continued as law and was decreed for anyone who contradicted a tenet of the group, and John Calvin (d. 1564) ordered Michael Servetus (d. 1553) to be burned at the stake in Geneva because he believed that innovations had entered the Christian faith prior to the First Council of Nicaea, as he used to say that the Holy Spirit animated creation in its entirety. So, his punishment was to burn over a fire until death, and likewise a scholar named Fainy was burned at the stake in Toulouse in 1629.

Martin Luther (d. 1546) was the staunchest critic of those who read the philosophy of Aristotle. He described the philosopher as 'the lying filthy pig', and similar nicknames which are unobjectionable as long as they come from religious zealots who are seeking to defend their faith. Calvin was less abusive to the philosopher than Luther, but he thought no better and was no more welcoming to one who read any of his works. Contrarily, Muslim scholars named this philosopher 'the First Teacher', so think of the difference between the two groups!

They [historians of Protestantism] said: Protestants called for intellectual freedom in understanding the Bible and for an abolishment of indulgences, which was the authority to forgive sins, the exchange of money for eternal happiness and reward, and, lastly, iconoclasm. But they did not budge in believing that the Bible is the beacon of guidance in the journey of human knowledge, just as it is the source of light for belief in the divine faith. It is not permitted for the thoughts of a sound mind to drive one to anything which contradicts anything contained in the Bible, and one has no need for any knowledge beyond that which it contains. In summary, they did not abolish a single principle from the aforementioned six principles; rather, they simply prevented the exaggerated authority of the rulers, which had been based upon the second principle.

They said: Consequently, the Reformist tradition was no less oppressive towards science and philosophy, and did not behave any better than the Catholics, because both traditions originate from the same nature – which is based on the six principles – and the only reward in both traditions for proponents of intellectual inquiry was death and the spilling of blood.

If I were someone who loved polemics in religion, I would have enumerated, in my discussion about the elements of the Christian religion, what is contained in the words of some of the critics of the Christian wars, and the oppression of the Church: 'How worthless is blood to the one who pretends to eat blood as an act of worship, and to the one who believes that salvation for humanity from sin is the shedding of innocent blood at the hand of a criminal sinner.' But, in this treatise of mine, I do not want to use the power of imagination, nor do I want to mention that which can be up for dispute. Rather, I will only speak of the indisputable state of affairs.

Separation of church and state in Christianity

All that remains for us to discuss is something which *al-Jāmi'a* considered fundamental to the split between religious and state powers, and by which the essence of the Christian religion claims to be tolerant towards science and philosophy.[20] If we concede that the phrase they quoted indicates a separation, as stated by *al-Jāmi'a* – and stated by many others who wanted to resist religious authority – then what would be the benefit of separation if the religion of the king itself necessitates enmity towards science and philosophy? Does the belief of the king and the spiritual salvation it propagates not prevail over the demands of the kingdom? And how many kings have sacrificed the welfare of their kingdom for the sake of their faith! Assuming that the welfare of the kingdom always prevails over belief and the strength of faith and love, and that the religion has established two separated powers, one of them to rule over the heavens and the earth in religious matters and the other to do so in worldly matters, then will this separation not lead to dispute between the two powers and demand each of them to overcome the other regarding that which is under their jurisdiction? Is it possible for the religious authority to allow its parish to be subject to the authority of the kings and for their bodies, wealth, and even minds to act for the welfare of a temporal kingdom, even if that behaviour is contradictory to the source of all knowledge, which are the divine books and the traditions of the spiritual leaders and their lives? If the religious authority intended to oppose this, could the other tolerate it? This is what has happened in the Christian world ever since the appearance of a religious authority.

How could it be possible for the state authority to overcome religious

20 i.e. 'Render to Caesar the things that are Caesar's and to God the things that are God's'.

authority and limit it within particular bounds when the religious authority derives its laws from God, and, due to that, its influence reaches the depths of people's hearts, it manages them as it wishes, and the king's only source of power is those people who are dominated by the religious authority?

It will not be possible for the king to oppose that power until he deals with the countless means to its authority. It is true that this separation could only facilitate tolerance if the bodies which are under the king's control could do their duties without the souls which give them life, and if the souls could also do their duties without the bodies which allow them to work.

Furthermore, is this really the meaning of the quote from the Gospel? The story, as it appears in the Bible, is that one of the hypocrites wanted to bring down the Messiah so he could execute his treacherous plan, so he asked: '"Is it lawful to give tribute unto Caesar, or not?" But Jesus perceived their wickedness, and said, "Why tempt ye me, ye hypocrites? Shew me the tribute money." And they brought unto him a penny. And he saith unto them, "Whose is this image and superscription?" They say unto him, "Caesar's." Then saith he unto them, "Render therefore unto Caesar the things which are Caesar's; and unto God the things that are God's."'[21] So, the clear meaning from the context of the story is: the one whose face is on the coins which you use for your transactions can tax you on them, and you must pay him the tax. But as for your hearts and minds and all else, they are from God and it is the mark of his work which is on them, so do not give any of that to Caesar. Knowledge is something which does not carry the mark of Caesar, but rather, it has the mark of God on it, so it is impossible for knowledge to be under any authority other than the spiritual authority. So, I ask, what kind of tolerance for knowledge is this?

Muslim belief about the Messiah and Christianity

Everything presented about Christianity's essence, its historical trajectory, and the interactions between its adherents and students of knowledge and intellectual pioneers throughout the ages until the present day was drawn from their own historical works and the sacred texts they depend upon to guide their conduct.

21 King James Bible, Matthew 22: 15–22.

As for my opinion, and the opinion of most Muslims, about the correct belief regarding the Messiah and his religion, then it is different from what the reader has seen so far. We believe that the Messiah was a mercy from God and His word and His messenger sent to the Israelites to affirm the Hebrew scriptures they possessed, so he came to them with a religion that contained guidance for them and right direction for their temporary and eternal affairs. He did not demand that they renounce any of the faculties which God had granted them, but he demanded that they show gratitude to God for them – a gratitude they could not express without utilising His bestowed faculties. The mind is the noblest faculty, or rather, it is the pinnacle of human faculties. Everything in existence is its scroll, with each page containing guidance from God and describing the path to Him; everything that we reliably know about the Messiah cannot contradict any of it. This is what we believe. If we have a reliable report about him which, in its apparent meaning, seems to contradict these principles, then it is possible for us to interpret it until its meaning conforms with those principles, or we simply leave the matter to God and say: 'We have knowledge only of what You have taught us. You are the All Knowing and All Wise.'[22]

The only religion is the religion of God, it is the one religion in the beginning and the end, and nothing changes about it except its manifestations and outward forms. As for its spirit and true essence, which all people have been invited to via prophets and messengers, then it never changes: belief in God alone, sincere worship of Him, mutual assisting between people to do good deeds and avoid harming one another. Faith progresses as the human intellect advances along with their readiness for complete guidance. We believe that the religion of Islam invited all of mankind with these principles, and its most critical function was to remove dispute between people who had received previous scriptures and to call them towards agreement, generosity, love, and unity. This is what the Muslims have done over the centuries, in accordance with their adherence to Islam.

If someone objects by asking: if what you have mentioned so far is an acknowledgement by eminent Europeans of the contradiction of Christianity's essence with science and philosophy, and its intense animosity

22 Qur'ān 2:32.

towards them, then what about the complete change that has taken place in Europe and the tolerance that it enjoys with those fields today?

Then the answer lies within the discussion about the fourth matter that *al-Jāmi'a* mentioned, which will come after a presentation of the essence of the Islamic religion, and what befits its relationship with science and philosophy, and what that essence led to, and then what was introduced to it and extinguished its glow, and what prevented its usual effect in recent years. We will summarise this as we summarised the above.

The Essence of Islam Towards Science and Philosophy in Accordance with its Principles

Introduction to the first principle

Islam, in reality, has two calls: a call to believe in God alone, and a call to affirm the prophethood of Muhammad.

As for the first call, it relies solely upon alerting the human intellect, directing it towards contemplating creation, implementing sound reasoning, and returning to the system and order which creation contains and the harmony between causes and effects, to arrive at the conclusion that creation is the work of the Necessary Existent, who is All Knowing, All Wise, and All Powerful, and that the Creator is one, due to the oneness of the system in creation. It frees the human mind to act in the way that its nature has facilitated for it without any restrictions, so it points out the creation of the heavens and the earth and the changing of night and day and the movement of wind – in such a manner so as to facilitate mankind to use it to subjugate ships for its own benefit, and the sending of those winds to move the clouds so that water may descend from the clouds and give life to the earth after its death, and whatever God wills is able to grow, such as trees and vegetation, which provides sustenance for the living and preserves his life – all of those are signs of God which are to be pondered in order to attain real understanding.

Then, Man can increase his awareness by remembering the foundation of existence, an element of which can be attained by an investigation into its realms, so he can think of how creation was in its earliest beginnings, as a Qur'ānic verse mentions: 'Are the disbelievers not aware that the heavens and the earth used to be joined together and that We ripped them apart, that We made every living thing from water? Will they not believe?'[1] And likewise in other verses, it provides free rein for the mind to run its course, which has been designated for it, on the path to arriving at the essence of creation. This awareness can also be increasingly effective in alerting the mind by that which is found in the traditions of the Prophet, as in the narration of the one who asked the Prophet: 'Where was our Lord before the heavens and the earth?' so he responded: 'He was in the clouds, below the air.'[2] One sees that the Qur'ān, in this important matter, does not confine the mind to what is mentioned in the Qur'ān, nor does it stop it at a certain point, or ask it to follow a certain formula. In fact, I will let the reader read the Qur'ān for himself and it should suffice in demonstrating how the Qur'ān invites one to contemplate the universe. 'Have they not contemplated the realm of the heavens and earth and all that God created ...'[3] 'There is a sign for them in the lifeless earth: We give it life and We produce grain from it for them to eat.'[4] 'Another of His signs is the creation of the heavens and earth, and the diversity of your languages and colours.'[5] There are other similar examples, and if I wanted to quote all of them I would have quoted more than a third of the Qur'ān, or even half of it, in this essay of mine.

The Qur'ān comprehensively mentions God's signs in the universe as a way to facilitate understanding, to remind one of blessings, and to engender thought, not to establish the laws of nature or to verify a specific doctrine amongst people. In providing evidence for monotheism, it does not stray from this path. Look at how striking the evidence is: 'If there had been in the heavens or earth any gods but Him, both heavens and earth would be in ruins.'[6] 'God has never had a child. Nor is there any god beside Him – if there were, each god would have taken his creation aside and tried to overcome the others. May God be exalted above what they describe!'[7]

1 Qur'ān 21:30.
2 Sunan Ibn Majah, Introduction, *Hadīth* 182. Quoted as 'He was in the clouds, below which was air'. This is the more common transmission of the saying than the one 'Abduh mentions.
3 Qur'ān 7:185.
4 Qur'ān 36:33.
5 Qur'ān 30:22.
6 Qur'ān 21:22.
7 Qur'ān 23:91.

So Islam, in this call and appeal towards belief in God and his Oneness, does not depend on anything other than rational evidence and human thought that works in accordance with the system of its primordial nature. So you should not be surprised by miracles, nor should you shield your eyes against phenomena which they are unaccustomed to seeing, heavenly calls should not silence your tongue, and your train of thought should not be stopped by a divine cry. The Muslims have agreed – except for a minority of them whose view is dubious – that belief in God takes precedence over belief in prophethood, and that belief in prophets is only possible after belief in God. Thus, it is incorrect to base one's belief in God on the words of prophets or divine scriptures, as it does not make sense to believe in scripture sent by God unless you have already affirmed the existence of God and that it is possible that He reveals scriptures and sends prophets.

Likewise, they say: the first obligation which every person is tasked with is to investigate and think in order to attain belief in God, and to then move from that to attaining belief in the prophets and the scriptures and teachings that were revealed to them.

As for the second call, it is the one which Islam verifies by way of miracles, and what can help you understand the kind of miracle Islam depends upon in its call to affirm the message of the Prophet? This miracle is one which has been mass-transmitted, and its effect is perpetuated. This is the one real piece of evidence, and every other report that has been transmitted – whether its narration is considered sound, well-known, weak, or baseless – Muslims do not consider any of these to be a source of unequivocal knowledge. Consequently, if any such report is narrated as evidence, then it only serves as supporting evidence to strengthen the conviction of the one who has accepted the core matter, and as extra support for those who accept those materials.

That mass-transmitted miracle which is depended upon as evidence to attain certainty of faith is the Qur'ān alone. The proof that it is a divine miracle and that it can only have been revealed by God – and is not the creation of a human being – is that it was conveyed by an illiterate man who did not know scripture nor was he a philosopher or a scientist. Furthermore, it was revealed uniformly as a guide to the misguided and a way to straighten the crooked and a support for the general system of life upon which one seeks guidance and a saviour from the loss they were in and the ruin they were on the brink of. Moreover, it is conveyed with a level of eloquence that no other speech can reach. So much so, that the rhetoricians were asked to oppose it with something similar and they were unable to, and they instead resorted to duelling with swords and shedding blood and persecuting the believers until they were forced to defend their rights. Then, truth prevailed over falsehood and the rays of Islam's sun extended to the corners of the earth, and its light spread across the world.

This miracle calls people to investigate it with their minds, and they are ordered to exert their utmost efforts in this investigation. If they find a way to negate its miraculous nature or its worth to serve as evidence for what it claims, they must present this. God says: 'If you have doubts about the revelation We have sent down to Our servant, then produce a single sura like it.'[8] And He said: 'Will they not think about this Qur'ān? If it had been from anyone other than God, they would have found much inconsistency in it.'[9] And He has said similar things, demanding they challenge the argument, and not demanding they merely accept without thinking.

The miracle of the Qur'ān combines speech and knowledge, and each one is dealt with by the intellect, so it is a miracle which is presented to the mind and has accepted the mind as a judge over it. It allows one to truly investigate it and disseminate its contents while maintaining its portion which never decreases. Thus, it is a miracle which has incapacitated any efforts to imitate it, but it still invited every capable person to try and produce whatever they can. As for the miracle of causing death without any conceivable cause, or resurrecting the dead, or exorcism, or faith healing, then these are only presented to those whose intellects have failed them and who lack understanding. God only brings these at the hands of His messengers to silence those who have allowed delusion to take over their minds and whose intellects have not been enlightened by the light of knowledge. As such, God establishes, with His power, and His signs for all people in accordance with their preparedness for them.

Thus, Islam does not use miracles as proofs of its claim to truth by anyone other than the prophets, and it does not indicate with a single word

8 Qur'ān 2:23.
9 Qur'ān 4:82.

that those who invite others to it have any capability to change a single thing in God's natural order – it goes without providing any proof for that, as it is too well-known to even require evidence.

The first principle of Islam: rational enquiry to attain faith

The first foundation upon which Islam has been built is rational enquiry, and enquiry is the means to sound faith. Thus, it grounds your footing upon it with evidence and summons you to reason, and whoever summons you to a judge has surely conceded his authority, so how can he dispute after that?

This principle was taken so far by the Muslims that adherents of the Sunni denomination said: 'The one who makes effort to investigate the truth but dies before arriving at it, whilst striving to attain it and not simply giving in to conjecture, will attain salvation.' What can be more accommodating than this?

The second principle of Islam: preference of reason over the apparent meaning of revelation when there is a contradiction

Before I move to another principle, I will begin by mentioning to you a principle which follows from the first: Muslims have agreed, other than a small insignificant minority amongst them, that if conclusive reason contradicts the transmitted details of revelation, reason is given preference. This leaves two possible approaches towards a transmitted detail: either it is accepted as a reliable transmission whilst acknowledging that it is impossible to understand, and the matter is then consigned to God and His knowledge. Or, we interpret the transmission in a manner that accords with the rules of language until its meaning corresponds with that which was affirmed by reason.

By this principle, which is based upon the Qur'ān, reliable tradition, and the practice of the Prophet, the door to reason is wide open. So, what space is spacious enough for critical thinkers and students of knowledge if this space is not? If there is not enough space in this for them, then no earth, with all its mountains and ravines, nor any sky, with all its stars and dimensions, can hold them.

The third principle: a principle of judgement in Islam: avoiding excommunication

Now we transition from these two principles to one which is popular amongst the Muslims and is known to be one of the fundamental rules of their faith: if someone says something that could be interpreted a hundred different ways to have been blasphemous, and there is only one way to have not been so, it is interpreted in the one way which precludes blasphemy, and it is not allowed to interpret it in any way that is blasphemous; have you heard anything from even the philosophers which is more tolerant than that? Does it befit any wise person to have reached such a level of ignorance that he says something which cannot be interpreted in a single way that is non-blasphemous? If he has reached this level of ignorance then it is best for him to face the verdict of a papal inquisition and to be taken by his hands and feet and tossed into a fire!

The fourth principle of Islam: consideration of God's universal laws in creation

The aforementioned principle of requiring proof for prophets' calls to guidance, disregarding reliance on miracles and supernatural phenomena, intersects with another principle which resonates with humanity's natural disposition, leading to a fundamental rectification of their actions in the Here and for the Hereafter, and that is the principle of considering God's universal laws with the people of the past and the present and the consequences of their actions.

The verses which have come in the Qur'ān to establish this principle are: 'God's ways have operated before your time: travel through the land, and see what was the end of those who disbelieved.'[10] 'Such was Our way with the messengers We sent before you, and you will find no change in Our ways.'[11] 'Do they expect anything but what happened to earlier people? You will never find any change in God's practice; you will never

10 Qur'ān 3:137.
11 Qur'ān 17:77.

find any deviation there.'[12] 'Have they not travelled through the land and seen how their predecessors met their end?'[13]

With this, the Qur'ān makes it clear that God has universal laws with all people that do not change, and established ways and practices by which matters are conducted and consequences follow, which are referred to as the laws of nature and some people call them rules; why should we be bothered about the difference in their phraseologies when the essence is the same? The Qur'ān calls to the communal human system and demonstrates that it results in one system which does not change, and anyone who seeks happiness in this community must look towards the principles of this system so that he can base his actions upon it and live in accordance with it. If one is ignorant of that, he can only expect despair, no matter how righteous or how pious he is. No matter how much one investigates or ponders, or searches and concludes, they will always conform with those universal laws. Those laws are in harmony with faith and faith is not antithetical to them, nor does it dissuade from studying them. Thus, why would it not demonstrate great tolerance towards them?

Islam came to eradicate idolatry – Arab, Greek, Roman or otherwise – in whatever shape or form it took or whatever name it was known by. But its scripture is in Arabic, and Arabic was the language of those idolaters. Understanding its meaning depended on knowing the conventions of the language, and its conventions could only be known by knowing the ways in which its words and phrases were used, and that could only be known by preserving the prose and poetry of the ancient Arabs, and these contained their customs and beliefs which provided one with a complete picture of their paganism and their idolatry throughout the ages. This is what the early Muslims did: they travelled and gave their lives whilst spending all their wealth in collecting, preserving, documenting, and explaining the words of the ancient Arabs, thereby attaining an understanding of the revealed book of their Lord, and they considered that a form of worship and hoped God would reward them for it. Thus, the essence of this faith does not denigrate any knowledge that existed in the time of its origin. Moreover, it could be a religious duty to learn things that are seemingly

12 Qur'ān 35:43.
13 Qur'ān 30:9.

unrelated to the faith, as long as one has a good intention for learning them, and this is a type of tolerance which is only considered valuable by those who are familiar with it. As for the early Christians, they dissociated themselves from the language of the Messiah, be it Syriac or Hebrew, and wrote the Gospels in Greek. Only the Gospel of Matthew was written in Greek, according to what has been relayed. Can you not see that the term 'Gospel' is itself Greek? That all happened because of their disdain for the Jews even though the Messiah spoke their language and sermonised them in their language – they shunned the study of their works and their customs.

The fifth principle of Islam: the overthrow of religious authority

The principle of Islam that I will now discuss – and what a magnificent principle it is – is the overthrow and utter annihilation of infallible religious authority.

Islam destroyed the edifice of that authority, and wiped out its trace, such that no name nor form of it remains for the masses. Islam does not allow anyone after God and His messenger to have authority over the beliefs of anyone or to control their faith. Even the Messenger of God was a conveyor and reminder, not an overpowering authority. God said: 'So [Prophet] warn them: your only task is to give warning, you are not there to control them.'[14] And it does not allow any of its adherents to permit or restrict the laws of heaven and earth. Rather, it frees the believer from any constraints upon him and leaves nothing between him and God except God alone, emancipating him from all forms of servitude except for God alone. No Muslim has a right, no matter how great his rank is in Islam, over another, no matter how lowly his station is in it, other than to offer advice and guidance. God says about those who are successful: 'Urge one another to the truth, and urge one another to steadfastness.'[15] He also says: 'Be a community that calls for what is good, urges what is right, and forbids what is wrong: those who do this are the successful ones.'[16] And He says: 'Out of each community, a group should go out to gain understanding

14 Qur'ān 88: 21–2.
15 Qur'ān 103:3.
16 Qur'ān 3:104.

of the religion, so that they can teach their people when they return and so that they can guard themselves against evil.'[17] Thus, the Muslims are mutual advisors and they are to establish a community which calls to goodness – they are the guardians over the rest – aligning the path if it becomes crooked, and that community has no right other than to remind and warn. It is not allowed for them or for anyone to seek out the inadequacies of another, nor is it permissible for the powerful nor the weak to surveil the belief of anyone, and it is not allowed for any Muslim to take his belief or base his actions upon anything other than the Book of God and the practice of His Messenger.

Every Muslim must understand God through His book, and the Messenger through his words, without an intermediary from the past or present. But he must first attain the means which will enable him to understand, such as: the rules of the Arabic language and its literature and conventions, the conditions of the Arabs, especially during the time of revelation, how the people were during the lifetime of the Prophet, what took place when the revelation was sent down, and some knowledge of the principles of abrogation. If one has not reached the station that will enable him to correctly understand the Qur'ān and prophetic practice, then he must ask those who have reached that station. Then, one should – rather, one must – demand evidence when he asks, whether his question concerns a creedal issue or a legal matter. Therefore, Islam does not have any semblance of what is known as infallible religious authority.

Civil authority in Islam

But Islam is a religion and a law; it has placed limitations and designated rights, and not everyone who believes in it acts accordingly. When desire takes over and impulses take control, rights are encroached upon and the encroachers go beyond the limits. Consequently, the wisdom of Islamic legislation cannot be actualised until the power to protect those limits has been established, the rulings of judges are able to be carried out, and the social system is protected. That authority cannot chaotically be held by a large number, it must be with one person – that is, the sultan or the caliph.

17 Qur'ān 9:122.

For Muslims, the caliph is not infallible, nor does he receive divine revelation, nor does he attain the exclusive right to interpret the Qur'ān or prophetic traditions. It is true that he must be able to practise independent *ijtihād*, that is, he must have attained knowledge of the Arabic language and the other disciplines – as mentioned earlier – so that he can understand what is needed from the Qur'ān and prophetic traditions to derive legal rulings. With this, he will be able to differentiate between truth and falsehood, integrity and corruption, and it will be facilitated for him to establish the justice that both the religion and the community demand of him.

He is not, due to this, allotted a particular merit or raised to a particular station by the faith due to his understanding of the Qur'ān or his knowledge of the law. Rather, he and the other students of religious knowledge are equal; they only outrank one another by virtue of the clarity of their intellectual prowess and their repeated successes in deriving legal matters. He is to be obeyed as long as he adheres to the correct procedure and the way of the Qur'ān and *Sunna*. Meanwhile, the Muslims remain in a state of observation; if he veers off course they guide him back to it, and if he acts in a crooked manner, they realign him with sincere advice and make excuses for him. There is no blind obedience towards a creation of God when he disobeys the Creator, so if his actions differ from the Qur'ān and *Sunna* they must replace him with someone else, as long as replacing him does not lead to harm which is greater than the benefit in removing him. So the community, or whoever speaks for the community, appoint him. The community is able to overrule him, and they can remove him from office when they see a benefit in doing that. Thus, he is a civil ruler in every sense of the word.

No rational person can possibly confuse the office of the caliph of the Muslims with what the Europeans call 'theocracy'. For them, that means he alone receives the law from God, he has the ability to legislate for his own best interest, and people are obliged to obey him, not via a pledge of allegiance or for the sake of justice and security in the land, but as a requirement of faith so that no believer who remains a believer may contradict him. One cannot believe that he is an enemy of the religion of God, even if his eyes have seen him act in a manner that does not accord with the religious law that he knows, because the words and actions of the religious authority, regardless of their nature, are: faith and law. Such was the authority of the Church in the Middle Ages, and the Church still claims this right, as mentioned.

One of the features of modern civilisation is the separation of state authority and religious authority, so the Church maintained the right to rule over beliefs and actions which relate to the relationship between a worshipper and his Lord: the Church legislated and abrogated what it wanted, was watchful and called people to account over whatever it wanted, and prohibited and mandated whatever it wanted. The state authority was granted the right to legislate in profane matters, matters related to people's conduct with one another, and they had the right to control anything which would preserve their societal system, in matters related to the Here, not the Hereafter. They consider this separation to be the source of all goodness.

As a result, they confuse Islam's decree that the two authorities are combined in one person, and they think that the way a Muslim interprets this is as follows: the Sultan is the one who stipulates the religion and the one who establishes its laws and ensures they are followed, and faith is a tool in his hand which he can use to make people's hearts submit and to appeal to their reason – thoughts and feelings are just possessions to him. Upon this, they imagine that the Muslim is bound to the Sultan by his faith, and they firmly believe that the Sultan opposed education and defended true ignorance, so it will not be easy for the religion of Islam to be tolerant of education as long as instating the Sultan remains a foundational necessity of the faith. It has been clearly shown to you that this is a blatant error and is far removed from the true understanding of that principle. You know that Islam does not have a religious authority, other than good counsel and the encouragement of goodness and of avoiding evil, and that is authority which God has bestowed to even the lowliest Muslim by which he can admonish the noblest Muslim, just as the noblest may do with the lowliest. Here, *al-Jāmi'a* can know that the office of the Sultan in the religion of Islam is not something to worry about nor to be a source of worry regarding the possibility of intellectual exploration. The previous essays have already alluded to the efforts of the 'Abbāsid, Umayyad, and Andalusian rulers in supporting knowledge and scholars, and we may add to this in that which follows.

They ask: 'If the caliph does not have that religious authority, then will it belong to the judge, the mufti, or the *Shaykh al-Islām*?'

I respond: 'Islam did not give these people even the least amount of authority over creed or law. All the authority held by one of the above is a civil authority that Islam granted them, and none of them can claim the right to control the faith of another nor the worship of his Lord, or to oppose him in his own path of inquiry.'

The sixth principle of Islam: protecting Islam by defensive war to avoid compulsion in religion

They say: 'Islam is a religion of holy war, killing has been sanctioned by it, and it has not been sanctioned in Christianity. Thus, a spirit of severity against anyone who opposes the religion is a part of its essence, and that is not the patience and forbearance which a peaceable law necessitates, which is what is found in many of the Christian commandments: "Whosoever shall smite thee on thy right cheek, turn to him the other also. And if any man will sue thee at the law, and take away thy coat, let him have thy cloak also."[18] Similar verses are found, such that even love for one's enemies has been commanded; it is not a choice, as with love for a friend. Rather, it is optional to balance between one's friends and enemies. However, in the Kingdom of God everything is possible and nothing is impossible.'

We say: 'Consider the following: is it only in Islam that one form of evil repels another when it alone is capable of doing so? Or, is it natural for one who has power to forgive his opponent? Killing is not a part of the essence of Islam; rather, it is part of its essence to forgive and overlook: "Be tolerant and command what is right: pay no attention to foolish people."[19] But killing is only sanctioned within Islam to repel the transgressions of rebels against the truth and those who adhere to the truth until they are safe from their evil, and peace can be secured against their danger. It is not to coerce people into the faith nor to take revenge against those who oppose it. This is why, in the history of Islamic conquests, you do not hear the likes of which you hear about in the wars of Christianity when the proponents of the "peaceable law" are able to fight those who oppose them, such as the killing of the elderly, women, and children.

---

18 King James Bible, Matthew 5: 39–40.
19 Qur'ān 7:199.

No Islamic battle took place with the intention of genocide, as happened in many battles at the hands of Christians wherein patience and peacefulness were only the adopted means when power and strength were lacking. The most that can be said is that divine care permitted Islam, in a short amount of time, to use force against its enemies in a way that had not been permitted for others in a long time, so it facilitated things for it in its adolescence that which was only facilitated for others in their dotage.'

Comparison between militaristic Islam and pacifist Christianity

In conquests, militaristic Islam was content with entering the conquered lands under its control and then allowing the inhabitants to continue their practices in accordance with their own beliefs in the manner required by those beliefs. It would only impose the poll tax which they would pay to secure their protection and preserve their safety in their homes, and they would, after that, be free in their beliefs, practices, and customs. They would not be troubled about their actions, nor would they be wronged. Muslim caliphs used to advise their military to respect the worshippers who separated themselves from the masses and remained in their monasteries solely for prayer, just as they protected the blood of women, children, and anyone else who could not engage in battle. Furthermore, there are mass-transmitted reports from the Prophet which prohibit harming the non-Muslims with legal protection living in an Islamic polity, along with a confirmation of their rights over the Muslims: 'Their rights and duties are the same as ours,' and, 'Anyone who harms a *dhimmi* is not one of us.' These continued to be actualised for as long as Islam had a position of power. I am not concerned if some Muslims disregarded these principles once Islam began to weaken – and meanness goes hand in hand with weakness; such mean attitudes have nothing to do with the nature and essence of Islam.

Pacifist Christianity considered it a right to dominate over the other religions that fell under its rule, and would closely monitor the acts of their adherents, singling them out with various kinds of mistreatment that none could bear, no matter how great their patience was. Ultimately, they would expel them, after having been unable to excommunicate or baptise them; they would evict them from their homes and wipe out any trace of them, as happened in all lands wherein a Christian community gained real control.

Nothing prevented a non-Christian from attacking a Christian except being outnumbered, or strong support, as witnessed by history and its writers. That is because Christianity did not come to bring peace, but the sword, and because it sets mother apart from daughter and son away from father. Whereas the scripture of Islam says even about disbelieving parents: 'If they strive to make you associate with Me anything about which you have no knowledge, then do not obey them. Yet keep their company in this life according to what is right, and follow the path of those who turn to Me.'[20] Even in its harshness against those who threaten peace, it does not require separation of father and son nor mother and daughter. Rather, it commands believing children to keep their company according to what is right in this life whilst preserving their religion.

Here you see that Islam, apart from the lands and people it conquers, is content with taxes that are less than those that they used to pay before they were conquered, and for them to live in harmony and not disturb the order of the polity nor infringe upon the system of the general authority. Then, it loosens the reins for them to make their own decisions regarding their private affairs, with nothing monitoring them except their own consciences. From another perspective, it forbids individual believers from cutting relations with their non-believing family members and demands that they treat them well. It is part of its essence to entrust people's matters to their Lord, and it is part of its essence to protect the one who does not believe in it and does not follow its practices, even if he is incredibly ignorant and misguided. Do you think, after all that, that it cannot tolerate science and philosophers, and that it has an issue with being gracious and generous with the one who spends his life establishing truth or elucidating obscurity or illuminating the path? Never! The one who researches, enquires, and studies, or travels the earth or reaches the heavens, will be safe from Islam concerning itself with any of his work, unless he incites rebellion or encourages misconduct, in which case the hand of the caliph will be extended to prevent any plotting, and to remove corruption by virtue of the faith itself.

---

20 Qur'ān 31:15.

The seventh principle of Islam: amicability of opposing beliefs

Marriage

Islam permits a Muslim man to marry a Christian or Jewish woman and gives her the right over her husband to remain in her religion, continue to fulfil her religious obligations, and go to her church or synagogue. In relation to him, she is a part of him that is as inseparable from him as his own shadow and remains his companion throughout all of life's ups and down, whether travelling or settled, the apple of his eye and the comfort of his heart, the queen of his house and the mother of his children, nurturing both them and him.

Islam does not differentiate between the rights of a Muslim and a non-Muslim wife, and the non-Muslim wife, despite her divergence in faith from her husband, is still included in the verse: 'Another of His signs is that He created spouses from among yourselves for you to live with in tranquillity: He ordained love and kindness between you. There truly are signs in this for those who reflect.'[21] Hence, she is entitled to her share of love and mercy even though she is not of the same faith. He seeks his tranquillity from her as she does from him, and he is as close to a garment for her as she is to him. Consider the ties of kinship through marriage between the families of the husband and the wife in the case of interfaith marriage, and the support and help between the two sides, as is found in human nature. How noble is the result of that between the children and their relatives? Do you not know how entrenched the ties of camaraderie are between Muslims and non-Muslims as a result of this? They serve as examples of a tolerance which has not been seen, either before it or after it, with the two preceding religions. It is obvious to anyone with clear reason that the establishment of tolerance in this way during the inception of the religion accustoms the heart to the feeling that the religion is about the relationship of the worshipper with his Lord, and creed is a condition of the heart which must be under the control of the Knower of the unseen alone, as He is the one who will call to account due to it. As for the worshipper, he cannot have any control over it, and the most that one who knows the truth can do is warn the one who is heedless, educate the ignorant, and guide the misguided, without giving a hard time to his partner,

21 Qur'ān 30:21.

subjecting her to any difficulties, leaving her unsupported, or going against the norms of loyalty and fidelity when dealing with her.

What do you think about a non-Muslim wife who is a person of strong intellect and adopts a way of thinking that opposes that of her husband? Would that decrease his love for her? Or weaken the feelings of kindness which God placed between them? If a Muslim is accustomed to toleration, or rather, love and support, for the one who opposes him in his creed, religion, and way of life, and he has accustomed himself to associating with him and helping him, then do you think that he will not tolerate seeing those around him contemplating the universe and arriving at a discovery or establishing a foundation for an art? If he can ostensibly differ from one who believes in or inclines to a view which is different to his, then will this not extend to one who he openly disagrees with, whilst he maintains the affinity which you have seen?

If I enumerated all of the elements and principles in Islam's essence which engender a disposition of nobility and represent true tolerance with scientific and philosophical inquiry, I would have written far more for the reader than what I already have. Thus, I consider it my obligation to conclude with mentioning a principle which I alluded to and which we must mention.

The eighth principle of Islam: combining the interest of this life and the hereafter

In Islam, life precedes religion. The commands of true monotheism, if it leads the worshipper to his Lord and fills his heart with reverence for Him and increases his hope in seeking Him, will not deter him from pursuing his living, nor does it prohibit him from enjoying his life, nor does it necessitate asceticism and leaving behind that which he enjoys beyond what is absolutely necessary.

The one who taught this religion did not say: 'Go and sell that thou hast.'[22] Rather, he said to the one who consulted him about what to give in charity: '[Give] one-third, and one-third is plenty. It is better to leave your heirs independent of means than to leave them poor and holding out their hands to people.'

22 King James Bible, Matthew 19:21.

The believers are obligated to fast, but if they fear sickness or an increase of sickness or there is incredible difficulty in it for them, they may leave it, or rather, they must leave it if they strongly believe it will be harmful.

Ablution with water is a condition of prayer, unless one fears some harm or faces difficulty in attaining water.

Standing is something that is an obligation for the prayer, unless the one praying faces difficulty in which case the obligation is revoked and then he may pray sitting.

Hastening to the communal Friday prayer is an obligation, unless there is heavy rain or anything which will cause difficulty in which case the obligation is revoked. In this context, you find the principle: a healthy body takes precedence over perfect religious practice. Thus, you see that Islam, in all its rulings, takes physical health into consideration, just as it obligates regard for spiritual health.

Islam has allowed its adherents to adorn themselves in several ways, and has multiplied the ways of enjoying desirable things, provided there is moderation and a good intention, and that it is within the boundaries of Islam, and befitting of an honourable character. The Qur᾿ān says: 'Children of Adam, dress well whenever you are at worship, and eat and drink [as We have permitted] but do not be extravagant: God does not like extravagant people. Say [Prophet], "Who has forbidden the adornment and the nourishment God has provided for His servants?" Say, "They are [allowed] for those who believe during the life of this world: they will be theirs alone on the Day of Resurrection." This is how We make Our revelation clear for those who understand. Say [Prophet], "My Lord only forbids disgraceful deeds – whether they be open or hidden – and sin and unjustified aggression, and that you, without His sanction, associate things with Him, and that you say things about Him without knowledge."'[23]

Then, God has considered beauty and adornment to be from amongst His blessings for us which remind us of His grace and drive us to remember and thank Him, as He said: 'And livestock—He created them too. You derive warmth and other benefits from them: you get food from them; you find beauty in them when you bring them home to rest and when you

---

23 Qur᾿ān 7:31–3.

drive them out to pasture. They carry your loads to lands you yourselves could not reach without great hardship—truly your Lord is kind and merciful—horses, mules, and donkeys for you to ride and use for show, and other things you know nothing about.'[24] Then He said: 'It is He who made the sea of benefit to you: you eat fresh fish from it and bring out jewellery to wear; you see the ships cutting through its waves so that you may go in search of His bounty and give thanks.'[25]

He established a law for spending and preserving wealth with His saying: 'Those who squander are the brothers of Satan, and Satan is most ungrateful to his Lord. But if, while seeking some bounty that you expect from your Lord, you turn them down, then at least speak some word of comfort to them. Do not be tight-fisted, nor so open-handed that you end up blamed and overwhelmed with regret.'[26]

The prohibition of excess in religion

One might fear that a believer may exaggerate in seeking the life to come and will cause his worldly life to go to ruin and, as a result, lose sight of himself in it. Therefore, He has reminded us – by narrating to us – that the life to come is attainable whilst enjoying the blessings of God in this world, when He said: 'Seek the life to come by means of what God has granted you, but do not neglect your rightful share in this world. Do good to others as God has done good to you. Do not seek to spread corruption in the land, for God does not love those who do this.'[27]

We see that Islam does not disregard the value of the tangible senses, just as it has prepared the soul to actualise its potential. He is the one who has constructed the various parts of mankind's essence, and thereby considered him a rational creature, not a mere body or a pure heavenly creation. Rather, He made them people of this world as well as people of the hereafter. He has kept them in this physical world whilst calling them to seek their spiritual fulfilment. Is that not what He elucidated in His saying: 'It was He who created all that is on the earth for you,' thereby loosening

24 Qur'ān 16:5–8.
25 Qur'ān 16:14.
26 Qur'ān 17:27–9.
27 Qur'ān 28:77.

the restraints surrounding their faculties, so that they may maximise their life experience?[28] Souls were made to compete with one another, and the love of competition for what they believe to be good, enjoyable, or beneficial is embedded within them.

It is against human nature to remain within limits when seeking something, or to stop trying to reach the very end of something. As such, God has specifically endowed Man with the capacity to progress through the stages of fulfilment in all ways that God wills him to progress, without any known limits.

The result of Islam's combining the interests of the religious and the secular

If the One who impels and draws souls, and guides and directs them, joins two desires: the desire to enjoy the things of this life and the desire to seek the perpetual blessings of the life to come, then He has brought everything together that could elevate them above a wanting life in this world and the dreadful punishment of the next. Thus, you see all souls proceeding resolutely with their hearts prepared, without fear of stumbling into punishment, nor cowardly trying to avoid searching for it. They seek things that will benefit them from this existence that they are in, and that was created for them, so they search high and low and are not content with parts over the whole. They search for its order, and they do not find anything which offends the eye in nature, and they search the waters and navigate by the stars, after learning their places and the course they take – their appearances and disappearances. In summary, everyone who is prepared in any way to inquire or penetrate a field of knowledge will be free to arrive at wherever his preparation allows him, either salvation or the realisation of some benefit or the completion of some enjoyment, and will not find anything in the faith that prevents him from his goal nor anything that will restrain him from his desire. How is this compared to that which sees no liberation except in repugnance of this knowledge and its uses, and finds that wealth and affluence are a cover that cannot be penetrated and come between one and the Kingdom of Heaven?

28 Qur'ān 2:29.

How can a Muslim truly thank God if he does not place the world in its entirety under the scope of his intellect, to penetrate its exterior and arrive at its interior and come to know its laws and principles, and use everything that can be used to increase its benefits? Does he really thank God when he does not fulfil such prerequisites? God has shown him, in His book and by the way of His Prophet, that the world was created for him, and God has placed it under the control of his intellect. Look at the affection of the allusion in the aforementioned verse: 'Who has forbidden the adornment and the nourishment God has provided for His servants?' until the end in which He states: 'This is how We make Our revelation clear for those who understand.' Thus, the real scholars are those who recognise the value of God's blessings by that which He has extended their sustenance, beautified their environment, and adorned their fineries.

Muslims are compelled by their faith to seek out that which will earn them prestige, leadership, honour, and glory, and they will settle for no less. None of that can be achieved without knowledge, so they are fully prepared to seek knowledge in all places, and they receive it through any hardship and in any language. If they encounter a scholar on any path, or stumble across one from any generation, or he appears to them from any tribe, they meet him with a cheery face, make all efforts to seek him out, and devote themselves to him. They are unconcerned about his creedal affiliations if they can benefit from his wisdom: 'Wisdom is the lost property of the believer, so wherever he finds it, then he is more worthy of it.'[29] Did their Lord not say: 'He gives wisdom to whoever He will. Whoever is given wisdom has truly been given much good, but only those with insight bear this in mind'?[30] Did they not hear His description of those 'who listen to what is said and follow what is best.'[31]

That is the relationship of Muslims with knowledge, if they are true Muslims; that is what the essence of their religion draws them to. There is a report that states, 'Seek knowledge even as far as China;' even if the report is not at the highest degree of authenticity, its meaning is mass-transmitted as it is found in the Qur'ān, as God has honoured knowledge

29 Sunan Ibn Majah, Book 37, *Ḥadīth* 70.
30 Qur'ān 2:269.
31 Qur'ān 39:18.

without any restrictions or specifications. Thus, the Muslim is commanded to seek knowledge even as far as China, and there were no Muslims in China during the era of the Prophet when he uttered that statement.

Knowledge is unique in that in the beginning one pursues it for other ends, but once one attains it, it becomes a pleasurable end in and of itself. You seek knowledge, firstly, out of a need to improve your lifestyle, raise your status, or defend yourself or your faith. Then, you soon find enjoyment in the knowledge itself, whereby the enjoyment in attaining it and arriving at its nuances become the ends that are sought for themselves and all other ends dissipate. The reason for that is obvious, as knowledge is the domain for inquiry and the intellect, and the intellect is one of the best human faculties, or rather, it is the best in truth. The All-Knowing All-Wise has made it enjoyable, just as he has allowed all other faculties to give enjoyment, and you do not need me to enumerate the enjoyments of sight, sound, scent, taste, and touch. Animals know that, just not Man. Every time the function of a faculty becomes greater in the slightest, its enjoyment becomes greater when it is used for its purpose, so it is possible for you to conclude from this that there is nothing more enjoyable to Man than discovering something unknown or deducing something logical. Islam has allowed for a Muslim to enjoy things in this world in a moderate manner. Is it not one of its enjoyments and the completion of its blessings that one can float through the ether of knowledge to gratify his intellect and traverse the earth to earn his living and support his dependants? In fact, knowledge was a necessity in the life of the Muslim, as we have mentioned, so if he begins to unpack its secrets and unravel its mysteries, it soon becomes his own leading desire and the one that distracts him from his other desires, until it becomes part of him, as happened with many Muslims. One of their great scholars said: 'We sought knowledge for other than God, but knowledge refused to be for anything other than God.'[32]

Outcomes of these principles and their effects on Muslims

Where did the essence of Islam steer Muslims? And what was its effect on their predecessors? ʿAmr ibn al-ʿĀṣ (d. 664) conquered Egypt and, with

32 ʿImāra notes that the scholar in question is Abū Ḥāmid al-Ghazālī.

his army, took control over Alexandria only six years after the Prophet passed away, or nine years according to some reports. Islam was still in its dawn and its light was spreading. One of the then-remaining pioneers of this period was a Christian man from the Jacobites whose was known as John the Grammarian Philoponus (d. 570). At first, he was a sailor who would pass by people in his ship, but he was inclined towards knowledge by his nature, so when a knowledgeable person would sail with him, he would listen closely to their counsel. Then, his desire for knowledge intensified, so he abandoned sailing and occupied himself with acquiring knowledge at forty years old, and he acquired it to an extent greater than one who had been studying since childhood. He became an expert in many fields, such that he was considered one of the leading philosophers, doctors, and logicians of his age.

Many Western and Muslim historians say: ʿAmr ibn al-ʿĀṣ heard about him and requested to see him. He honoured him due to his knowledge, and a friendship developed between them which became famous, until one Western philosopher said: 'The friendship contracted by Amrou [sic], the conqueror of Egypt, with John the Grammarian, indicates how much the Arabian mind was predisposed to liberal ideas. Its step from the idolatry of the Caaba [sic] to the monotheism of Mohammed prepared it to expatiate in the wide and pleasing fields of literature and philosophy.'[33]

Muslims mixed with the inhabitants of Persia, Syria, and southern Iraq, and included them in their duties, and Islam did not stop them from using them for this, such that the language of administration in Syria was Greek and did not change to Arabic for decades. Thus, thoughts intermingled and the tolerance of the faith led to Muslims studying sciences, literature, and craft.

Muslim engagement with literary and rational sciences

Twenty years after the death of the Prophet, the Caliph ʿAlī ibn Abī Ṭālib (r. 656–661), may God honour him, encouraged the teaching of Arabic literature and requested that the rules of grammar be codified when he saw

33 The original in Arabic here is a direct translation by ʿAbduh of Draper, see *History of the Conflict*, p. 105.

that there was a need for that. The Muslims began to fully experience the light of knowledge in the darkness of those trials in accordance with the demands of their faith and its revealed law. Even if their civil wars, which had been ignited in the corners of their lands over the disputes about the matter of the caliphate, distracted them from many useful things, they never distracted them from seeking knowledge and studying it systematically in accordance with their natural disposition. Proficiency in literature included knowledge of Arab history as well as poetry and eloquent prose. During the caliphate of the Umayyads, this reached a level that no community has since replicated. The Umayyad caliphs knew its worth and raised the ranks of the poets, orators, and historians, such that the effects of the rational sciences appeared in the far corners of their empire, and a number of rational and practical books were translated by the end of the first century.

The Umayyad caliphs moved the centre of the caliphate from Medina to Syria, and they did not practise the asceticism that the rightly-guided caliphs did. Once, a messenger from Persia came to see ʿUmar ibn al-Khaṭṭāb (r. 634–644), God be pleased with him, and when he asked about him, he found him sleeping under a palm tree amongst the impoverished. However, when the messengers of rulers came to see Muʿāwiya (r. 661–680), God have mercy on him, he was in a lofty palace which had been adorned and built in the most exquisite manner available to the Arab craftsmen, full of gardens and water fountains and furnished with the best of furnishings, such that one would see the most elegant décor. Yet, with that, Muʿāwiya had not contravened the faith nor deviated from its path, as he only made use of that which was permissible, and enjoyed the concessions God granted him. Of course, this included the promotion of a myriad of innovative artistic abilities.

Their engagement with cosmology at the beginning of the second century

The Umayyad state, and its inhabitants, fell upon a number of misdeeds, as we have mentioned, and it was followed by the ʿAbbāsid state, which established itself on its attribution to the family of the Prophet around the end of the first third of the second Hijri century – 132 H (749). Al-Manṣūr moved the capital to Baghdad, which then also became the capital of science and civilisation, and al-Manṣūr began also to establish schools for medicine and law. He then dedicated some of his time to the study of astrology. His grandson Hārūn al-Rashīd completed what he began and ordered that every mosque have a school attached to it for studying numerous disciplines. Then al-Ma'mūn came and the state of knowledge reached its apex and produced its greatest riches. It is said that he brought so many books to Baghdad that it took a hundred camels to carry them. One of the conditions of his treaty with Michael III (r. 856–867; a Byzantine emperor known for restoring the use of icons in the Byzantine Church and for leading successful military campaigns against the Arabs and Slavs) was for him to give one of the libraries of Istanbul, and he found a valuable work of Ptolemy in the field of mathematics and astronomy. Al-Ma'mūn then ordered for it to be translated and called it the *The Almagest*. It is not easy for one to count the number of various scientific books translated under the 'Abbāsids, the children of the uncle of the Prophet.

Their development of public and private libraries

Islamic regions began to take an interest in libraries in an unprecedented manner, such that Cairo, in the early fourth century, had a library which contained 100,000 volumes, 6,000 of which were about medicine or astronomy. It was a part of the system for them to be loaned to students living in Cairo. There were two globes in it, one of which was made of silver, which some say was built by Ptolemy himself and he spent 3,000 dinars on it, and the second was made of brass. The books in the library of the caliphs in Spain reached 600,000 volumes, and its index was forty-four volumes. They found that Spain alone had seventy public libraries, and these contained spaces specifically for referencing, copying, and translating.

Some elites used to be enamoured with books, and made their homes educational institutes due to what they contained. It is said that the Sultan of Bukhara called for an Indonesian physician to visit him and was told it was not possible as his books required 400 camels to carry them and he could not do without them. Hunayn ibn Ishaq, the Nestorian, was one of those in Baghdad who had made his home a public library, which students of the rational sciences and mathematics would frequent, and he would generously give his time to them.

Their development of colleges for sciences and the method of teaching within them

Colleges covered the broad face of the Islamic world. We say this despite its size because it increased in scope beyond that of the Roman Empire, as you would find colleges in every region: with the Mughals, with the Mongols in the East, in Marrakech, in Fez, and in Spain in the West.

The method of teaching used by the teachers was for each one to prepare his lesson, then he would write whatever he wished about the topic he would teach, then he would deliver the class to his students and they would take notes, then these lessons would become books and lecture note compilations which would be published amongst people across disciplines. We hasten to note that historians have agreed that all articles and books were published and studied by people without even a negligible level of surveillance or censorship or removal of anything that was written by the author, other than one historian whom I have seen mention that a law was established in some Islamic empires that required books of theology to only be published with official permission, although I do not know of a single instance in which that happened in an Islamic empire when Islam was truly Islam.

We return to our points about the Islamic colleges: Gibbon, when speaking of Muslim preservation of knowledge in the East and West, said:

> The same royal prerogative was claimed by their independent emirs of the provinces; and their emulation diffused the taste and the rewards of science from Samarcand and Bochara to Fez and Cordova. The vizier of a sultan consecrated a sum of two hundred thousand pieces of gold to the foundation of a college at Bagdad, which he endowed with an annual revenue of fifteen thousand dinars. The fruits of instruction were communicated, perhaps at different times, to six thousand disciples of every degree, from the son of the noble to that of the mechanic: a sufficient allowance was provided for the indigent scholars; and the merit or industry of the professors was repaid with adequate stipends.[34]

34 Edward Gibbon, *The History of the Decline and Fall of the Roman Empire*, Vol. VI, Chapter LII (Reprint, London: W. Baynes & Son, 1823), p. 485.

At one time, there were three Islamic empires and three claimants to the caliphate: the 'Abbāsids in Asia, the Umayyads in Spain, and the Fatimids in Africa. The competition between the three of them was not limited to matters of territory and rule, but was strongest in the fields of science and literature. The observatory of Samarkand that was established in the East shows the care they paid to astronomy, and the observatory called Girald in Spain was a response by the people in the West to show that they had no less concern.

All the colleges in the Islamic lands based their examination curriculum in the colleges of medicine on the medical college in Cairo, which was the most exacting and precise curriculum, and no doctor could practise medicine until he had attained a degree demonstrating his success in the examination, with its rigour. The first medical college established in Europe with this curriculum was the one established by the Arabs in Salerno in Italy, and the first observatory established in Europe was the one built by the Arabs in Seville in Spain.

The Muslims were enamoured with the cosmological sciences in all their diversity, and in arts and literature with all their variety, even imaginary folklore tales about all social circumstances, and began taking knowledge from Greek and Syriac and soundly translated works of the early masters from those languages into Arabic. In the beginning, their translators were Christians, Sabiens, and others, and then many Muslim scholars learned Greek and Latin and wrote dictionaries of those two languages, and that was just to take the sciences from their roots and shift them into their language according to what they knew of them. Also, at first, the teachers of the children of the aristocracy were Christians and Jews. And then the colleges and universities were developed and the professors in them were from all religions, each one teaching the field in which he was known for his expertise.

Western sciences and their discoveries

At first, the knowledge of the Arabs was Greek, but it only remained so for a century until it became Arab as the Arabs were not content to remain mere students of Aristotle, Plato, Euclid, or Ptolemy for an extended period of time, as the Europeans did for ten entire centuries.

They said: 'Roger Bacon was the first to advocate for empiricism in modern sciences, or that, with it, he replaced mere transmission from teachers and sticking to ancient views, and thereby emancipated knowledge from the shackles of blind imitation.'[35] That is true for Europe, but as for the Arabs, this principle was established amongst them at the end of the second Hijri century.

The first thing which distinguished the Arab philosophers from philosophers of other nations was their epistemological reliance on empiricism, and not being content with rationalism, such that Gustave Le Bon (d. 1931) quoted a European philosopher in stating that the principle of the Arabs is: 'Test, observe, scrutinise, and you will learn,' whereas for the Europeans after the tenth century, it was: 'Read from books and repeat what the professor says, and you will then be a scholar.' Thus, Egyptians and other Easterners must notice how the situation has reversed, and how bad the result has been.

Delambre said about the history of astronomy: 'If you can count two or three Greek astronomers then the number of Arab astronomers is innumerable.' In chemistry, you cannot find a single empiricist among the Greeks, whereas you can find hundreds from the Arabs. Thus, chemistry is considered an invention of the Arabs. Geometry, arts, and mathematics were considered to be logical tools used to deduce theoretical issues, and they are the most reliable means for deducing new insights, as is known.

Arabs were the first to use an astrolabe to reckon the time, and they were the first to master the use of the water clock for this purpose.

They also discovered the laws of measuring weights, solid and liquid, such that they established charts which were incredibly precise and reliable, just as they did so in astronomy. Those charts were well known and were consulted by astronomers in Samarkand, Baghdad, and Cordoba, such that those laws were close to the discovery of the law of gravity.

I am not able to enumerate all of the Arabs' discoveries in this essay of mine, nor the numerous sciences which they developed, as that would require a large volume, and the fair-minded and knowledgeable European philosophers and historians have already done so, and perhaps the upcoming Arab generation can circulate that to their compatriots so that they

35 We were unable to locate a source for this quote.

can learn what their ancestors achieved. However, I will quote something, which was stated by one of the Western philosophers:

> Sometimes, not without surprise, we meet with ideas which we flatter ourselves have originated in our own times. Thus our modern doctrines of evolution and development were taught in their schools. In fact, they carried them much farther than we are disposed to do, extending them even to inorganic or mineral things. The fundamental principle of alchemy was the natural process of development of metalline bodies. "When common people," says Al-Khazini, writing in the twelfth century, "hear from natural philosophers that gold is a body which has attained to perfection of maturity, to the goal of completeness, they firmly believe that it is something which has gradually come to that perfection by passing through the forms of all other metallic bodies, so that its gold nature was originally lead, afterward it became tin, then brass, then silver, and finally reached the development of gold; not knowing that the natural philosophers mean, in saying this, only something like what they mean when they speak of man, and attribute to him a completeness and equilibrium in nature and constitution – not that man was once a bull, and was changed into an ass, and afterward into a horse, and after that into an ape, and finally became a man."[36]

The philosopher Gustave Le Bon said: 'The Arabs are the ones who taught the world how freedom of thought is compatible with the integrity of the religion.'[37]

Here, I disagree with some of the philosophers who have stated that Ibn Rushd's belief in free thought led him to contravene the essence of religion when he said: 'The individual souls do not remain when the body dies, but what remains is the universal soul.' This is an error due to their misunderstanding of his speech in explaining the eternality of the genus, but not individual souls. Yes, Aristotle and others said: 'People live and die but the genus remains.' They also erred in saying about him: 'He believed

36 Draper, *History of the Conflict*, p. 118.

37 'Abduh seems to be paraphrasing from Le Bon's *La civilisation des Arabes*. See Gustave Le Bon, *La civilisation des Arabes* (Reprint, Paris: Le Sycomore, 1980).

that God was the essence of the world manifested in its composition and everything ultimately merges into Him, leaving nothing else in existence.' This is similar to their aforementioned view. Ibn Rushd was a Muslim who knew Islam is not inconsistent with philosophy, but it does negate this type of delusion, which is adopted by those who stumble in their pursuit of knowledge. Many who were intoxicated by this view recovered from it. But the extant books of Ibn Rushd make it hard for us to attribute this view to him due to what I have mentioned, but I do not disagree with its attribution when attributed to Ibn Sab'īn (d. 1271), who studied with Ibn Rushd's students, as some of his statements do allude to that.

Another philosopher said:

> The sciences which the Arabs inherited from the Greeks and others were lifeless between book covers, buried in library walls, or stored in certain minds as if they were precious stones in a treasury, people's share of it was mere gazing from afar. But for the Arabs, they became the lifeblood of their literature, the nourishment of their souls, the essence of their fortune, the backbone of their craft, and the spur which drove human innovation to all that it was made for. There is no European who has studied history and exercised his intellect that denies the credit for removing Europe from the darkness of knowledge to the light of knowledge, and for teaching it how to investigate and think, and for showing them that empiricism is the basis upon which real knowledge is acquired, the credit for all of this goes to the Muslims and their literature and their knowledge which was taken to Europe and entered Spain, Sicily and southern Italy, and France. It was a blessing for Arab knowledge and Muhammadan literature that they came to Italy when the Pope was absent, as his seat had been moved to Avignon, France for approximately seventy years. Knowledge spread into Sicily and southern Italy and remained there. The streets of Paris were not furnished with stones until the twelfth century, and it then had pavement like that of the cities of Spain.

Another said: 'I do not know how, over a period of two centuries, Islam gave us an innumerable number of astronomers and the Church controlled the Christian world for twelve centuries in Europe and did not produce a single astronomer.'

This intellectual progression was not limited to a single class over others. Rather, everyone was able to take part in it equally, with the only difference being effort and output. This is due to the deliberateness of the caliphs and their associates, and the tolerance of the faith and its ease on its adherents and those under its protection. One Western philosopher said something which is known to be true and corroborated by empirical data: 'No nation in the world ever saw a conqueror who had this level of deliberateness, nor a religion which reached this level of malleability and benevolence.'[38]

Caliphs and rulers taking scholars and scholarly production by the hand

The caliphs, about whom it is said: 'They are the religious and political leaders simultaneously,' would themselves study the sciences and invite others to do so. They were governors and scholars. The caliph al-Ma'mūn would sometimes persecute enemies of the philosophers, and history has known many famous names who spent months or years in prison because they opposed philosophy, thinking that it contained elements that opposed the faith or would corrupt it. Have you seen a religious leader of another faith who persecuted people who opposed learning and those who were harsh against the philosophers? Perhaps you will never find such an example.

Scholars and men of letters, in general, were respected amongst the caliphs and rulers and were treated as they deserved. Take the example of Abū al-ʻAlāʼal-Maʻarrī, due to his notoriety amongst the masses for his borderline heresy.

ʻAlī ibn Yūsuf al-Qifṭī (d. 1248) mentions that Ṣāliḥ ibn Mirdās (r. 1025–29) – the ruler of Aleppo – went to al-Maʻarra, whose inhabitants had disobeyed him, so he clashed with them in a siege and launched catapults at them. When the people of al-Maʻarra felt defeat, they sought aid from Abū al-ʻAlāʼ ibn Sulaymān – Abū al-ʻAlāʼal-Maʻarrī's nickname

38 ʻAbduh's source for these quotations remains unknown.

– and asked him to intercede for them. So he went out with his commander. Ṣāliḥ honoured him and asked: 'Do you need anything?' He responded: 'The ruler – may God grant him a long life – is like a cutting sword, it is like the day that is blistering hot and is malleable, but it soon cools.' He then quoted the verse: 'Be tolerant and command what is right: pay no attention to foolish people.'[39] Ṣāliḥ said: 'I have given it to you.' And then said: 'Compose some poetry which we can recite.' So he spontaneously composed some verses about him, and Ṣāliḥ left. See how the ruler spared a city whose inhabitants disobeyed him, due to a philosopher.

If I mentioned everything that scholars and philosophers received from rulers and caliphs, this article would be far longer than it already is, and what I have mentioned should suffice.

Removing two doubts and explaining the reality of so-called persecution

Some people have erroneously thought that persecution is manifested in the hatred of the masses and the lies they create against people of pure reflection and free thought, and their whispering and winking amongst one another about such people and their mocking of them with nicknames, or even demeaning them in certain instances. This does exist in Muslim history, but it is a clear error because this type – of one who dislikes free thinkers – is present in all places no matter how free its inhabitants are and no matter how knowledgeable they may be. Those who adhere to Catholicism in France, until today, hate philosophers who openly oppose the Church and write against their principles, and Catholic groups fabricate lies about things they never said, and declare that looking into their writings is impermissible in religious law. We do not doubt that similar to this existed amongst Muslims in the days when the market of philosophy was thriving, but this is not persecution at all. Rather, it is people's disdain for that which they do not know, but then they leave them and go about their own business.

Others have stated: 'History tells us that some leading thinkers were put to the sword due to the excessiveness of their thoughts, so no freedom

39 Qur'ān 7:199.

was left for them to enjoy. And it would be incorrect to deny that which the caliph al-Manṣūr and others did with the heretics.'

I say: 'Many excesses, if they spread amongst the masses, disrupt their order and violate their safety, as was the case with al-Ḥallāj's (d. 922) views and those like him. The authorities were forced to intervene in the matter to preserve the safety of the masses. So they arrested a man of thought, not because he exercised his thought but because he did not want to limit his right to freedom. Rather, he wanted to limit others to his perception of freedom, although others had no need for what he saw as his right. Persisting in excessive claims to freedom may lead to dissension. Accordingly, those in charge of preserving order think that society must be purified from these kinds of people to protect its foundations from being shaken. We see today that secular philosophy afflicts religion with this type of persecution. Did the French government not compel the priests and monks to have their organisations and schools operate under governmental authority? They could not take any initiative without the permission of the government and anyone who did not abide by that would have his organisation disbanded and his school closed by the power of the sword and they would be exiled from the land, as many were exiled in preceding years. Yet, is this called persecution? Never. Rather, real persecution is the persecution of the Inquisition and the persecution of the leaders of reform after it first began.'

What will they say? That education for Muslims was rare or hidden, a mosque or a school which was attached to a mosque wherein a jurist, a theologian, a scholar of *Ḥadīth*, a grammarian, a philosopher, an astronomer, and an engineer would sit. A student would move freely from the jurist to sit in front of the philosopher, and from a class of *Ḥadīth* to a class on ethics. If a debate took place on a particular issue, freedom of thought prevailed based on persuasion and a compelling argument, while zealotry diminished within the deliberations and tolerance predominated.

'Amr ibn 'Ubayd (d. 761) was a leading Mu'tazlite and one of the staunchest in following the principles of the School. Nonetheless, he was a teacher of Imām al-Bukhārī, author of the *Ṣaḥīḥ*, and he also had a high standing with al-Manṣūr, such that he once said to him: 'I have silenced others with gifts, but not you.' Thus, look at how an Imām of the Sunni creed has his chain of narrators connect with a leader of the Mu'tazlites and sees no issue with that.

If one thinks about those who opposed certain men of learning, who suffered from harshness in Islam and were killed by the stupidity of the kings due to the incitement of jurists and extremists in faith, then one must look at their contexts. One will immediately notice that those who incited them were not driven by mere religious fanaticism, nor by a desire to preserve the faith and make a lesson out of them. Rather, you will find that jealousy was the primary cause of all of that, and faith was simply an instrument for it. This is why you only see such cases of punishment meted out to chief judges like Ibn Rushd – and al-Ḥākim's pardoning of him and his reinstating of his position are proof of that – or a vizier or a caliph or a sultan, or one who holds sway over the masses. Such is the case with the jurists who sought to harm the philosophers, and when some jurists sought to destroy others, as could be seen by eye-witnesses and is narrated to us by history. As such, this is not to be considered from the meaning of religious persecution against philosophy, as envy amongst one another is something that is found within those who have no real faith, despite adhering to its outwards forms. Comparatively, that type of persecution is the one that is motivated by a mere disagreement in creedal matters, or the supposition that one has contravened the faith in a matter of knowledge or action due to the insufficiency of the faith to accommodate within its fold one who differs. This did not happen in Islam, unless there was such an instance that has not reached us.

This is the nature of the Islamic faith that is evident in its most basic elements and the constituents of its essence. This was its effect in the Eastern and Western world. This embodies the expansiveness of the faith's favour, its ability to tolerate dissent, and its providing of refuge to those who have differed to take shelter in it when they seek its shade. Is there anything hidden about this? Would a rational person be pleased with himself if he denied such radiant enlightenment? Does Islam not offer a wry smile, whilst in the most intense state of worry over the potential faithlessness of its youth, to a cultured person whom it does not take as an enemy, even if it does not consider him a friend, when it sees him take aim at it and stray in his judgement over it?

Islam today and judging Islam based on Muslims' conduct

One may ask and say: 'We concede that Islam's essence is against the persecution of real knowledge, and no torture nor burning at the stake took place amongst the early Muslims, nor was anyone hanged for studying cosmology nor for advocating for human rationality. However, are the Muslim scholars of today not opposed to rational sciences, and contemporary arts, and do the masses not follow them in this?' Would a cultured person not have an excuse for what he sees and hears around him? Would he not have heard that a man from a Muslim land other than Egypt wrote an article about *ijtihād* (independent reasoning) and *taqlīd* (imitation) and arrived at the same conclusion that all Muslim scholars did, and an article in which he elucidated his view on Sufism, stating that it was of no benefit to Islam, rather it harmed it? Or he stated something similar to this – which is something that was done by the majority of Sunnis before him. So when his article was published in Egypt under his name, those who don turbans and wear the garments of scholars were furious with him, saying: 'He has renounced the true faith and has presented obvious falsehood.' Then, his matter was raised to the governor, who had him arrested and thrown in jail. His appeal reached the capital city of the empire and he asked the Sultan to order his transport to the capital to affirm his innocence from the lies against him, in front of an equitable person who does not stray, who stands by the truth and does not rule unjustly, and so on and so forth until the end of his appeal. Then, his call was answered, but none of that helped him, as the order was given for him to be jailed there also and he was not pardoned until many months passed, despite not saying anything except that which accorded with the foundations of the faith which no reader nor writer would rebuke, nor anyone else.

Have people not heard that Shaykh al-Sanūsī (1859) – father of al-Sanūsī of al-Jaghbūb – wrote a book on the principles of Islamic law in which he added to certain topics in the principles of the Mālikī school of jurisprudence? There is an allusion in his book to his claim that he is one of the people who can derive laws from the Qur'ān and prophetic tradition directly, and he had opinions which contradicted that of a *mujtahid* or two. One of the Mālikī scholars came to know of this, and he was a leading professor at Al-Azhar University.[40] Consequently, he took a spear

40 This is in reference to Muhammad 'Ilish (d. 1882).

and intended to stab al-Sanūsī with it as he had torn apart the sanctity of the religion and followed the path of the heretics. Perhaps the professor would have dared to stab al-Sanūsī with it had he encountered him, and the only thing which saved al-Sanūsī from it and protected the dearly departed professor from the evil consequence of that and from having committed a crime in the name of the religious law was al-Sanūsī's departure from Cairo before the Mālikī professor came across him.

Have people forgotten the long articles that were published in newspapers for almost three years by some Azhari scholars, expressing their disapproval of the inclusion of geography amongst the subjects which the students of al-Azhar would study? The authors of those articles opposed anyone who indicated that this subject should be included with those ones, and that they wished to detract from the religious sciences.[41] Were chapters not published last year by some of them which aimed to defame one who dared to criticise certain creeds, despite him not uttering a censorious statement nor saying anything which distanced one from the Qur'ān or prophetic practice?

Have people not narrated to us the situation of the scholars of Afghanistan, India, and Iran, and the way they adhere to ancient customs and cling onto that which they have inherited from their forefathers, such that they declare war against anyone who tries to distance them by the span of a single finger from the practice of their predecessors, even if adhering to that will lead to their destruction? And the situation of the current Moroccan government and their extreme partisanship and punishment by dismemberment for smoking, or by death for stating something which listeners find reproachable, even if the early Muslims would have all agreed with it?

Can one who ponders not imagine a future with much noise, uproar, and disturbance if it is said that the students of al-Azhar must study some of the fundamentals of science or that they should study natural history? Would the pious-minded not resist it? Would they not all shout out: 'This is an attack on the religion and a weakening of its stable core. It is a deception off all its poor adherents'? And they would persist in saying this, sparing no usage of words found in Arabic dictionaries to dismiss it as an innovation.

41 It was 'Abduh himself who advocated for the inclusion of geography in the al-Azhar curriculum and subsequently faced criticism.

Is this condition new for Muslims, such that one could say it is a condition which has only recently afflicted them or an illness which has newly infected them? Someone who has closely observed the state of Muslims over the course of centuries would preclude the notion that this state is a sudden affliction affecting communities, given that its manifestations are so ubiquitous. If you take a Muslim from the Atlantic coast and one from behind the Great Wall of China you will find them both saying the same thing: 'We saw our fathers following this tradition; we are only following in their footsteps.'[42] And all of them oppose anyone who differs from them, even if he quotes the Qur'ān or gathers all of the *Ḥadīth*.

A group have claimed that they have shaken off the dust of blind conformity, and removed the veil that stood between them and a direct reading of the Qur'ānic verses and prophetic traditions to understand God's commands from them without an intermediary. But this group is even more narrow-minded than the conformists, despite having rebuked many innovations – and they have removed many things from the faith which were added to it – as they considered it obligatory to act upon what is literally understood and restrict oneself to that, without looking to the principles on which the faith is built and to which the Islamic call was made and for which prophets were sent. Thus, they were not supporters of real learning nor were they devotees of peaceful civilisation.

It is hard not to criticise the rigidity of the jurists and their attachment to the words of preceding authorities, despite their differences and the varying opinions in understanding them. If an incident takes place and there is no view from a well-known author about it, they will refrain from providing an opinion and will try to change it from its real nature to something that conforms with an accepted statement from one of their books, such that one student from an Ottoman region wanted to join one of the schools of al-Azhar until a doubt arose: 'Does his region qualify to be included within the will of the one who provided the endowment?' So someone said to the Shaykh of the school that the books of geography affirm that his region met the condition of the one who provided the endowment. He said: 'I am not convinced by what is in those books, rather the correct thing for me to rely on would be a deceased jurist who said this region is from this

42 Qur'ān 43:23.

territory and it is included within the endowment.' If it were said to one of them: 'If the community had itself specified certain areas without drawing up a map for us detailing the inclusions of each region and the borders which each ends at, then the principles of our faith allow us to draw upon the statements of scholars in this field – who are part of our community – by mass-transmitted reports and similar clear pieces of evidence', he would respond: 'I want a legal text, not a rational argument.'

It might be said to them: 'The situation has become complex, and people's presumptions and dispositions have become corrupt whilst their actions have become amoral. Their beliefs have strayed and their acts of worship have lost the spirit of sincerity, so they commit evil acts against one another. Most have been seized by poverty, so their strength has deteriorated. Honour has become degradation, guidance become misguidance, need has become a housemate, and necessity, a trusted friend, and you still suffer from all that afflicted you and the masses; has that inspired you to research the ways that your ancestors followed, and the reasons why you and people in general have ended up where they are?' They will say: 'That is not our duty nor did God obligate us with that. That is for the rulers to look into and to search for the means to remove it. If they are unable – and they will be unable – that is because it is the end of times, and reports have been transmitted which indicate that it is an inevitable reality, and Islam must be lifted from the earth and the final hour will take place for the vile ones.' They rely upon Qur'ānic verses and prophetic reports for their despondency and despair and do not inspire any action.

Renan's view on Islam

This stagnation – which, if we wanted to explain how it extends to the depths of thoughts and emotions, we would need to write an entire book about it – is what led Ernest Renan, the famous French philosopher, to say in his presentation about the tolerance shown by different religions towards science that *al-Jāmi'a* quoted:

> Although I fear that the Islamic faith will establish itself in the face of this general tolerance of different creeds, I know that some men who adhere to the ancient etiquettes of the Islamic faith, including

> men from Persia, have good seeds, which indicate open-mindedness and intellect that inclines towards tolerance. Though I fear that these seeds will be suffocated by the dogmatism of some jurists, and, if they dissipate, it will be the end of Islam. This is because there are two certain matters: Firstly, modern civilisation does not want to eradicate religion altogether just because religion cannot be a means to it. Secondly, it will not accept religion to be an obstacle in its path. Thus, these religions must be more malleable, or their demise will be necessary.

So where does this general stagnation come from, which allows critics to rule that Islam is an obstacle in the path of Muslims that trips them up before they can be successful in their efforts or attain victory through their works, if it is not from the essence of the faith? And what is the cause of the events which we narrated if they do not stem from the foundations of the faith? Even if you do not concede that this is persecution and that persecution is an integral part of the Islamic faith, then you must at least concede that it is animosity towards learning, or a dislike of it, or a condemnation of it, or a belittling of its status. Any one of these conditions is sufficient – if it becomes common amongst the Muslims – to cause them to lose all glory and stave off any benefit, and to actualise what Renan and others have warned about. So how do you respond to this?

The response

I say: 'This statement has some truth to it, and it also contains an element of reality. As for what we hear around us from the prison of the one who simply quotes the earlier generations, the one who seeks to attack him is not one who is himself steadfastly holding onto the faith. Rather, the campaign of the turban-wearers was spurred on by envy, not protectiveness over the faith. As for the imprisonment, it relates to politics and the fear that a single thought will escape from the chains of blind imitation and will spread, such that it will alert someone who was heedless, and then a third will follow, and then the issue may spread from religious issues to other issues … until the very end of free thought (from which they seek refuge in God).'

You might want to say: 'Politics persecutes thought or religion or learning, then I am with you as a witness to this. I seek refuge in God from politics, and from the mere word politics, and from every letter in the word politics, and from every thought that occurs to my mind about politics, and from every land in which politics is mentioned, and from every person who speaks or studies or reasons or goes mad about politics, and from every possible grammatical conjugation of the word politics!'

A proof that the imprisonment was political is that the person was advocating the view of the early generation of this religion. Do not tell me that this type of politics is religious. I seek the witness of God, His messenger, His angels, and all our predecessors, that this type of politics is a matter that is far removed from religion, as if it were the tree that: 'grows in the heart of the blazing Fire, and its fruits are like devils' heads. They will fill their bellies eating from it; then drink scalding water on top of it; then return to the blazing Fire. They found their forefathers astray, and rushed to follow in their footsteps.'[43]

Muslim stagnation and its causes

As for the stagnation which I described after that, then it is incorrect to attribute it to Islam. You have already seen Islam in its purest state; there is nothing in it which is a source for what I have mentioned, nor the dangerous consequences which Renan and others have warned of. Rather, it is a sickness which infected Muslims once other ideologies seeped into their hearts and dwelled alongside the faith of Islam within them. The reason for them having control over Muslims and for extinguishing the light of Islam from their minds is politics. Likewise, it is that cursed tree mentioned in the Qur'ān – obeying desires and following the path of devils is politics.

I have never seen a religion whose foundations are preserved while its people have been confused about it more than Islam, like a king who was abandoned by his army, his treaty was not respected, his promises and threats were not taken seriously, his vision was unclear to the heedless ones even if it was clear to those of insight, his ancestors were taken by death and his offspring were like cattle. They did not understand it such

43 Qur'ān 37: 64–70.

that they could establish it, nor did they care about it, so they abandoned it. Equals connected to it, associated themselves with it, and stated: 'We are its adherents, its tribe, its protectors,' yet they had nothing to do with it, except something akin to the connection ignorance has with knowledge, or fickleness has with forbearance, or a fool has with one of sound judgement.

Look at how a distinguishing feature of Islam became a reason for what its adherents did. Islam was an Arabian religion, then it associated itself with science and philosophy, so these became Arabian science and philosophy after they had been Greek. Then, a caliph erred in his policies when he used the scope of Islam as a means to do what he thought was best for him, thinking that the Arab army could help an 'Alawid caliph, because the 'Alawids were the closest relatives of the Prophet. He wished to assemble an army comprised of non-Arabs, such as Turks, Daylamites, and others whom he thought would be beholden to his authority and be won over by his benevolence, so they would not support anyone who opposed him nor help anyone who sought his place. The spacious scope of Islamic law allowed him that, and that is when Islam became non-Arab.

An 'Abbāsid caliph wanted to assemble for himself – and how badly it turned out for his community and his faith – a foreign army, and he promoted leaders from within the ranks. Before he knew it, the army leaders mutinied, and assumed authority over him, and control of the polity fell firmly within their grasp. They did not possess the intellectual prowess that Islam condones, nor the heart which faith refines, and they did not engender any sympathy. Many of them used to worship other gods in secrecy, and only prayed with the congregation to solidify their power. Then, others committed injustices against Islam, such as the Tartars and others who took positions of leadership.

What enemy could be worse for these people than knowledge which teaches people their real value and uncovers their poor standing? So they were hostile to education and its close associate: Islam. As for knowledge, they did not pay any heed to its proponents and did not allow it any support, so they placed their own supporters within the ranks of the scholars and made them take their appearance so that they could be considered among them. Then, they manufactured things about the faith which made them despise education and removed the desire to seek it. They entered upon them – whilst being heedless – from the door of piety and preservation of the faith, and claimed that the faith was deficient so that they could complete it, or it was sick so they could treat it, or that it was declining so they could prop it up.

They looked at the ostentation of the paganism from which they hailed and the customs of the Christian communities that were around them, so they borrowed from them a false exaltation for Islam's rites and a veneration for its decrees; barbarians support tyrants and are the hand of the oppressor. Thus, they created festivals and groups for us, and established for us the worship of scholars and saints who were similar to those that fragmented the community and made people regress to their initial state of misguidance after having been guided. They decreed that a later scholar may not say anything that had not already been said by an earlier one and made that into a dogma, such that thought stopped and intellects congealed. Then, they spread their supporters across the Islamic kingdoms to propagate stories, reports, and opinions to convince the masses, and any matters that concerned the community and the state must be looked at by the rulers and no one else, and anyone else who concerned himself with these matters was involving himself in something that was not his business. Also, any apparent corruption or adverse state of affairs was not the fault of the rulers but was instead the realisation of prophecies that spoke of the state of the world at the end of time, and there was no way to rectify these matters and the only safe option was to consign these matters to God, and a Muslim must only concern himself with his own affairs. They found support in the apparent wording of some *Ḥadīth* – unreliable and fabricated *Ḥadīth* were extremely helpful for spreading these delusions.

An army of these misguided individuals spread among the Muslims, and despotic rulers across the lands supported them. They used the doctrine of predestination as a way to hinder ambition and chain people to restrict them from doing deeds. Naivety was the strongest factor in convincing people of these fantasies. Religious insight waned and caprice coincided with matters that, if they came together, would cause destruction, so the truth was obscured under the darkness of error. Contradictory beliefs became entrenched in the public psyche and the principles of their faith diverged from the straight line, as is said.

This type of politics – of tyrants and ego-maniacs – is the one which propagated things which entered the faith that were alien to it, and stole the hope from Muslims, which could have taken them beyond the heavens, and replaced it with a state of hopelessness adjoined with barbarity. Hence, that which the laity calls Islam is not really Islam. All that has been preserved from Islamic deeds are the outwardness of prayer and fasting and pilgrimage, and a few words which have been taken out of context. Thus, people have reached – due to the innovations and fantasies their faith has faced – the state of stagnation which I mentioned, and have considered it faith. We seek refuge in God from them and from their lies against God and His religion. All that Muslims are criticised for today is not Islam; it is something else they have called Islam. The Qurʾān is a true witness: 'It is an unassailable Scripture which falsehood cannot touch from any angle, a Revelation sent down from the Wise One, Worthy of All Praise.'[44] It bears witness that they are liars and that they do not take it seriously and opposed what it was brought for. We will complete the discussion on the ills of this stagnation for you, and we will prove that it is an illness which must be lifted.

The ills of this stagnation and its effects

This stagnation has persisted due to the efforts of those who are invested in preserving it, and they have been enthusiastically defending it, and many ills have resulted from it which would take time to explain, so it is best to summarise it:

Faith is that which leads the intellect to the vast landscape of knowledge, and with it, it spreads across the earth and reaches the heavens to see a sign of God or unveil a secret of creation or extract a law of its system. Every art form serves as a stage for the intellect to extract the benefits it seeks and derive as much enjoyment as desired. When faith stagnates, and pursuers of truth do nothing, knowledge stagnates and the wind of its momentum settles. This does not happen all at once: it happens over stages.

44 Qurʾān 41: 41–2.

The crime of stagnation against language

The first crime of this stagnation was against the Arabic language, its expressions and literature. People were interested in it due to their faith's need for it. Their need to understand their scripture required knowledge of the language's subtleties and the allusions of its constructions. They found that they could not attain that until they became like Arabs in their grasp of the language, equal to those who are Arabs by nature. So when the successor only relied on the words of the predecessor, there were fewer people who could understand what was said before them, and they were content with accepting God's word as a bequest without referring to its proofs. If they did look at the proof and found that it did not support the understanding held by their predecessors owing to a mistake on the side of such predecessors by virtue of their fallibility, they would deny what they saw and would blind themselves and say: 'We seek refuge in God from our minds thinking that which our predecessors did not,' and they would compel their minds to stop, which would afflict them with paralysis in that regard. After that, what need would there be for the Arabic language itself? They would be content with enough of the language to understand the structures of their predecessors' words, and yet these were not the Arabs whose words the earliest generation would look to.

Similarly, every successor is inclined to limit his understanding to looking at the words of his predecessor, and does not concern himself with the earliest predecessors, nor with the context in which their predecessor lived. He only looks at the wording, so his rank in attaining the language drops in relation to his distance from the early masters of the language, until the state of people reached what we see today – they have designed lessons for understanding expressions of certain authors in books of grammar and rhetoric, even if they do not achieve the goal of understanding anything else. Hence, knowledge of the early generation eroded and their sciences declined. In fact, books of earlier generations were lost, may God be pleased with them, so the one who is researching the *Mudawwana* of Mālik or the *Kitāb al-Umm* of al-Shāfiʿī, may God have mercy on them, or some of the primary books in Hanafi law, has become like the one who is searching for a Qurʾān in the house of a heretic. He will find part of the book in one corner and another part in a different corner, and if the parts are all brought together for you, you will find that all the typos of the editor are a barrier between you and attaining any benefit from the text.

This is all a result of stagnation, thinking poorly about God, erroneously believing that the gates of God's bounty were closed in the faces of later generations in order to raise the ranks of prior ones, and not taking heed from the *Ḥadīth* that state that the one to whom knowledge is conveyed may understand it better than the one who first hears it, and that this community is like rainfall: it is not known whether its beginning or end is best. Not taking heed of that has led to the contributions of the predecessors being lost! Indeed, everything is powerless without God's support. Undoubtedly, the reader has comprehended the level of harm this crime has had on the language. Sufficient proof of that is, if one speaks his language, the language of his religion, scripture, and community, he will barely find anyone who can understand him, and what harm could be worse than preventing the meaning of one's speech from reaching people's minds?

The crime of stagnation against order and society

Greater than this crime is the crime of division, breaking apart the order of the community, and causing it to fall into the differences, divisions, and depravity in faith that others before it fell into. The difference among the earliest generations in their legal opinions was due to the different understandings of individuals, with each of them relying on a single source, which they did not disagree about, that is, the Qur'ān and reliable reports about the Prophet. As such, there were no guilds nor groups nor dogmatists opposing other dogmatists, and if one of them were to find that what another said was true, he would hasten to agree with him, just as many of them had expressed. Then, proponents of stagnation came and said: 'A child born in the house of a man from the school of a scholar has no right to switch from the school of his father to another one.' If you questioned them on this, they, paying lip service to this difference, would say: 'All of them have a share of the Prophet of God.' But this was merely stated by the tongue and had no basis in the heart. Then there were battles of contestation between the scholars of different legal guilds. Had they used their power and resources in clarifying the foundations of the faith and spreading its etiquettes and sound matters of creed amongst the masses, we would be in a different state than the one we find ourselves in today. One who looks over the books of those who differ and criticise one another will find that which is not permitted by any fundamental principle of the faith to which they ascribe themselves. They accuse each other of misguidance and throw accusations against one another of being removed from the faith, and the criticiser is no better than the one being criticised. But this is the nature of stagnation: it often leads to stubbornness.

The differences in theology were like those in law, individuals differed in their views and conclusions, and each group benefited from the other and did not pay any heed to their differences in opinions. Their mosque was one, their *Imām* was one, and their preacher was one. Then, stagnation played its part – the part of politics – and people who differed began to nitpick, and the prayers then became disunited, groups were distinguished, and factions formed. That all went against what the faith called for, and certain people even put in their effort to truly distinguish between the groups but were unable to, as the distinctions were all illusory and were mostly based on differences in phrasing. Certainly, rivalry and different forms of politics ignited the fires of wars between those who ascribed to different factions, until the matter resulted in this division, which one would think there is no cure for.

One stated a few years ago: 'It is necessary to appoint judges in Egypt from the four legal schools, because the principles of these guilds are similar and the expressions in their texts are easy to understand.' One also said: 'The need to follow the laws in some of the statements of the school of Mālik or al-Shāfiʿī is pressing, in order to grant ease to the population and stave off any harm or corruption.'[45] Consequently, many of the supposedly pious began lamenting and bemoaning the luck of the faith, as if the one seeking the above was seeking something foreign to the faith, even though he was only seeking the faith itself and only followed that which accorded with the faith, and perhaps people had already acted upon this all over the world a few years before the current norm. So where is their saying: 'All of them have a share of the Prophet of God'? Rather, it is the stagnation of the successor towards the view of the one who directly preceded him, and his refusal to look towards anything else. Or, it is

45 ʿImara notes that ʿAbduh is alluding to his own prior suggestions here.

politics, which permits and prohibits whatever it pleases, and strengthens and weakens whatever it pleases, and the masses are driven to it by the reins of power and desire.

The crime of stagnation against religious law and its proponents

This stagnation in Islamic law led to difficulties that consequently caused people to ignore it. The Islamic legal system – in the days when Islam was truly Islam – was tolerant and encompassed the entire world, whereas now it restricts its own adherents, such that they are compelled to draw on other systems and to seek the preservation of their rights under systems that are surpassed by the *Sharīʿa*. However, even the pious ones would resort to non-Islamic systems to get their disputes resolved.

Dealing with Islamic law has become so difficult for people that they are content with remaining ignorant about it due to their inability to act upon it. Thus, you do not see one who truly knows it except for a few, which is nothing compared to those who do not know what it is. Hence, how could it be expected from one who is ignorant of the *Sharīʿa* to act upon its teachings? Consequently, most of the masses have fallen into contradicting their legal system. Moreover, they no longer respect it, because they can no longer act in accordance with its dictates. The first preventative for them is the difficulty in understanding it due to the complexity of the expressions and the large number of different opinions.

I once asked a teacher of one of the legal schools: 'Do you buy, sell, and utilise your wealth according to what you find in the books of your legal school?' He responded that it was rare for those laws to occur to him when he was involved in such dealings; he would simply act in accordance with what everyone else did. This is what stagnation did to its people, and if they wanted to give life to the *Sharīʿa* so that people could live by it, they would have done so, and it would have been easy for them and for others to have lived through it.

You know where people have ended up in terms of poor manners and violating the boundaries of the *Sharīʿa*. If you asked for the reason in towns and small cities, you would find that it comes down to two matters: either the loss of a knowledgeable person who knew the law and the faith, and the fall of the town or city into the foolishness of ignorant people, with them asking one another about the lawful and the prohibited, whilst the one who is asked knows no more than the one asking as all of them are ignorant. Or, the one who knew was unable to explain to the one who asked him as his tongue was unable to clearly speak in a manner that the laity could understand. If asked, he read from a book and recited an expression which was difficult for the listener to understand and for the speaker to explain due to the constraint he placed upon himself, so he was not able to act upon that which he heard nor what he knew. You might tell a knowledgeable person: 'Learn methods of communication that will enable you to communicate with people from different strata so that you can benefit others with your knowledge, and elevate yourself so that you can understand the purpose of your *Imām's* words so you can find an application in his principle for this issue through an example.' But if he does not find this precise issue mentioned in his words or in the words of his followers who came after him, he says that he does not want to introduce anything that his teacher, whom he studied directly with, did not mention. If he were to broaden his vision, he would find that previous scholars had already done so and had conveyed it, such that they contradicted the one whom they learnt from in some of his views. Then, if you disputed him on these grounds, it would not be far from his thoughts to consider you a heretic and that you are calling him to apostatise. Yet the poor man does not realise that, in that, he is contradicting the tenets of his faith and that he is opening the door for apostasy. We seek God's refuge.

I once had a conversation with a teacher about advising students and reminding them of the virtues of good actions and ethics, especially when delivering a lesson to them about law, prophetic teachings, or theology. He said to me: 'There is no purpose in doing that at all and it is an unnecessary burden.' I said to him: 'It is your duty to urge what is right and forbid what is wrong, not to dominate and compel them nor to ensure they never do wrong.' He said: 'If it has become impossible to benefit, then urging and forbidding are just vain talk.'

Thus, see how he believed in the impossibility of benefiting from his advice due to the absolute spread of corruption among people, as he claimed. But he did not look for a way to remove this corruption even though his faith calls him to do so. And yet he worked daily to teach those he had no way of reforming. That is all because he did consider himself capable of adopting a means that the one he learnt from did not adopt nor guide him towards when he was in front of him. During that time, he did not remember any of the divine commands about advising and urging one another to do good and forbidding one another from wrong, and that despair in God's grace is only found in disbelievers or misguided people.

No, if you said to him: 'This type of teaching is an illness which will not produce the desired result,' or 'This book which the students are used to reading is harmful to the reader, and there are others which are better,' he would think your words here contravene the faith. Yet, a fair-minded person would see that what he had accustomed himself to was a violation of the faith, and he may declare war against you, thinking himself a righteous combatant in God's path by doing so.

You might say to him: 'The classes of our earliest predecessors were to establish rulings and to dictate facts to the students, and none of them had a book in his hand which he would make the students read, and the students only had their pens and parchments to write down what they heard from the mouths of their teachers.' He may confess to the truth of your words, but he would persist in his actions based on what he found people doing. So, does an intelligent person really think that this stagnation is from the faith? Does one with even the slightest insight doubt the dire consequences of this for the faith and its adherents?

The crime of stagnation against theology

That is these people's stagnation regarding deeds, but even more harmful is their stagnation in theology: they forgot that which is in the Qur'ān, supported by the practice of the Prophet, which states that faith depends on certainty and that it is not valid to rely on conjecture in this regard. Furthermore, it states that the intellect is the source of certainty in the matter of faith in God – knowing it and having the ability to believe in it – and affirming the revelation. Tradition is the source for what follows from that regarding knowledge of the Unseen, such as the Hereafter, and for forms of worship. Also, even if the intellect alone does not suffice in discerning a matter that is necessary from within the tradition, then it certainly suffices in believing in God's existence and that He sends prophets whom we learn the tradition from. They forgot all of that and said: 'One must follow a specific school of thought in theology.' They split themselves into groups – as we said – and they were not content with following a specific school in a particular creedal issue, but some of them stated that one must accept specific evidence to arrive at that creedal issue. Thus, it is as if their conformity is a conformity of inference, as if they have made tradition the pillar of all beliefs. If only it had been the tradition of the Prophet, but it is tradition even if from an unknown person and so a principle has been established for them: belief X is correct because the book of so-and-so says it is. When the books differ from one another, it becomes difficult for one to find pure, unshakable belief. That is the case with the illiterate people who follow the conformists; you find them believing in everything that has been said and relaying from a well-known person, even if he is not an expert in the field itself. Their beliefs contradict one another based on the contradictions of what they have heard.

Leniency in relying upon tradition has led to a divergence from the project of the *Salaf*, God be pleased with them. They used to examine the qualities of those they narrated from and would test their sayings until they arrived at near certitude that they were reliable. But the stagnation of the successor regarding that which reaches him from a predecessor has caused the tradition to fall into chaos, such that you find everyone relying upon those whom they know while assuming they are appropriate to be relied upon without any investigation or research, until sayings and fabricated reports have become so widespread amongst people that voices are sometimes raised in opposition to them. All the recurring innovations you see originate from the false belief that was born out of careless conformity, stagnation in restricting oneself to what an earlier person stated without any research into his evidence nor examination of his state, and a neglect of the intellect in creedal matters, in opposition to what the Qur'ān and prophetic practice call for. For this reason, beliefs have been adopted that require much effort by one who wishes to protect the faith by removing them, and his ammunition is the Qur'ān whereas the ammunition of his enemies is the sayings of known and unknown people from the past. Many people support his enemies today, but this number will be far reduced tomorrow, by God's will.

Someone asked the Grand *Imām* of al-Azhar about the ruling of an act that takes place in the mosques on Fridays – and the *Imām*'s leadership amongst scholars of the religion is clear – the *Imām* answered according to what goes in line with the *Sunna* and to what is known by the scholars who are deeply rooted in the tradition. So, he said: 'It is an innovation which must be avoided.' Do you think that the questioner could act upon this verdict? No! What happened was a lot of gossiping and many questions were raised, and politics played its role. Then it was said: 'Time will support the truth, and this is the way we came across the issue.' The questioner quieted down, and what could the responder do?

Yes, this is from the misfortune of that stagnation. It has drawn a line between the laity and those from whom reform is hoped for. They entrusted people who had no knowledge, neither of faith nor literature, who firmly implanted evil seeds into the minds of the masses which produce unpalatable fruits for the community. If a scholar of the religion attempts to clarify God's clear law from His book and the practice of His messenger, that which all of the *Salaf* agreed upon, he would be shouted at in his face by a lay person: 'We never heard this from our forefathers.'[46] By his forefathers, he means those he saw after his birth or he heard their names mentioned by those who misled him, such that guiding the masses has today become one of the hardest matters and the most difficult for the one seeking it.

What can I say? In seeking to worship, man has committed some of the most egregious crimes in the faith. If he is called to abandon one of those crimes, he will stomp and yell and be obstinate and arrogant. Look at what those obsessed people, and those like them, do when it comes to purifying themselves from urine before the eyes of passers-by, and there are women and children amongst them, and they think that they are drawing closer to God by doing this.

This is the state of the masses. They see that which is not faith as faith, and it is difficult for those whose job it is to protect the faith to guide them due to the masses' rigid commitments to what they inherited from those who inspired them without any thought.

This is the majority of the community whom you can see slipping out of the hands of their warners, and if they wanted they would each approach their own companions, which is the easiest thing for scholars of the *Sharīʿa*. This would simply be a return to the tolerance and receptiveness

46 Qurʾān 28:36.

of the faith that was prevalent with the Prophet and his companions and then working to preserve it and keep it alive.

Stagnation and the students of formal state education

Then this stagnation created another group for us: students of modern education, either in the Muslim state schools or in the foreign colleges in their countries or outside of them. I am not speaking about this group in Crimea, the Caucasus, Samarkand, Bukhara, or India as I do not know a lot about their contexts, and I have seen goodness in every one of them I have seen. I hope that, through them, their people will actualise what Islam has been waiting for from those who know it, for I have seen few individuals from those who studied in European countries and have meticulously studied sciences there and they are more committed to the essence of the Islamic faith and its spirit than many of those who call towards devotion and piety. They do not allow themselves to abandon a true custom that their faith has bequeathed to its people. These are wonderful students, may God increase their number.

I am only speaking about the students in Egypt, Syria, and the other Ottoman regions from this group. Islam's tolerance and its open-mindedness towards learning allowed Muslims to send their children to study in official and unofficial schools from Muslim and non-Muslim teachers, or from all non-Muslim teachers. There are schools which were only built to spread a faith other than the Islamic faith and they allowed the parents of the non-Muslim students to remain silent about them and to not critique their system, as long as their creed remains safe from destruction and debilitation.

The quality of the students in foreign schools

These students, if they are in foreign schools that have no trace of teaching the Islamic faith or even teach another faith, have developed some weakness in their beliefs. In some cases, their faith disappears altogether, and other beliefs take their place and contravene them, as has been seen repeatedly. If their fathers had attained knowledge of their religious beliefs due to convincing reasoning, they could have supported the beliefs of their children and preserved what was shaken or what disappeared altogether. However, how can those fathers have any of this knowledge when stagnant ancient methodologies are used, which are barely understood by those who are fully dedicated to knowledge, let alone these poor souls? If there were people who could guide them to a methodology that is easy to understand, it would facilitate these students to be guided by their faith. But stagnation has made everything difficult and every matter impossible.

This crime of stagnation against Muslim children who study in foreign schools disconnects them from their faith in ways that they cannot comprehend. If only they exchanged the religion with other sources of literature and wisdom that may refine their characters, as some deluded people who do not know the nature of such a community hope for, or as some who want no good for our community hope for. But it has left their hearts empty of every preventative or impetus other than a preventative for good and an impetus for evil. So, they have taken their desires as a deity and their cravings as a teacher; they destroy themselves and others. Among these are the wealthy inheritors whose shameful and evil deeds are prevalent in the newspapers every day. Undoubtedly, ignorance is better than what these people study. If only Islam had not welcomed the likes of this harmful education.

Stagnation of students in official and national schools

As for the students in official and unofficial schools for religious education, they developed some understanding of various disciplines, which taught them truths about astronomy, geography, or even sociology. Anyone who comes to know about something will talk about it, and a foolish person who wears the garb of a religious scholar could hear it while he is fixed upon words he has previously heard. When he hears anything else he rebukes it and assumes that it contradicts sound creed. Thus, he will start to blame the student, rebuke him and accuse him of disbelief, while the student will not doubt the strength of his evidence and, due to his ignorance of the faith, will believe that what his interlocutor says is a true representation of it. Thus, he will flee from the faith as one flees from ignorance. If one were to say to him: 'Consult the religious texts and you will find what pleases you and will help you against yourself and your interlocutor,' he would be in a state of confusion and not know which book to consult. He will struggle to understand the expressions that his predecessors have left behind due to their complexity and obscurity – and they had simply preserved them the way they found them – so he will return to fleeing from the faith as one who seeks to understand flees something which cannot be understood.

Due to this, most of these students believe that the religion is something which cannot be understood; some of them may even consider it mere legend. Hence, they sideline it, and disregard its beliefs, virtues, and culture while seeking the culture of another, which they rarely find. Consequently, you see them and their hearts have cooled and their ambitions have ceased such that they only seek what the masses seek: livelihood and status. They seek that by any means, even if it means harming the laity or the nobility – as long as honour is preserved. If one of them is found to claim nationalism or denominational concern or the like, he will publish words which do not reference a reliable source or sound knowledge. As a result, he calls for that which is beneficial for his country in a way that actually leads to harm, knowingly or unknowingly. Some of them cry out in the name of the faith, yet they are not moved to learn any of its laws or creedal articles. They do not practise what they preach, and dishonesty permeates everything they do. If it were not for this stagnation they would have found, in the texts of their religion and in the sayings of those who conveyed it, that which would gladden their hearts and content their souls and they would have tasted the seasoned flavour of religious knowledge and they would have been able to benefit themselves and their people. There would have been a known group among them who would be consulted in matters of the community, their political thought and societal actions.

Stagnation is an illness which can be cured

Detail of the harms and evils of this stagnation would require an extended treatise so we will be content with what we have summarised in the previous pages. Nonetheless, what remains is to discuss that it is a fleeting disease, which can be done away with, if God Almighty wills.

You know that it is the essence of the Islamic faith – from what has been presented to you above – to rise above any attribution to this malignant disease – the disease of stagnation. How plentiful are the verses of the Qur'ān which rebuke the blind following of ancestors, regardless of their grand achievements, and which call for exercising rationality regarding their practices and beliefs? It is needless to repeat that.

Then we also alluded to some of the causes which brought this stagnation upon Muslims – not upon Islam – and that its originator was either an adversary of Muslims who sought to lower their rank or enslave them and chain them up for himself, or was an ignorant ally who thought well but acted poorly. The latter is more egregious and a greater facilitation towards error. Will this illness subside and Islam return to its initial tolerance and bountiful generosity in a way that makes Muslims benefit from its riches?

The Qur'ān says: 'We have sent down the Qur'ān Ourself, and We Ourself will guard it.'[47] That is the Qur'ān 'whose verses are perfected, then set out clearly, from One who is all wise, all aware.'[48] As the Qur'ān stated: 'Scripture whose verses are made distinct as a Qur'ān in Arabic for people who understand.'[49] God promised to preserve this Scripture and His promise has been perpetuated; neither the hand of a combative advisory nor of an ignorant ally can reach it, so it has remained as it was revealed. It is safe from the fallacies of those two groups; it remains between its covers, clean, pure, and free from argument and disputation. It is the *Imām* of the pious and the repository of the faith. It is the recourse when times are tough and people have fallen prey to misguidance; its rays of light still pierce through the veils that others have erected, and its supporters must tear those veils down so its light can shine for the eyes of its protectors, God willing.

This light continues to shine in the depths of darkness for individuals to whom God granted insight, so they are guided by it and towards it. They praise the course they are upon as they know the success of their efforts. But as for the ones who have had the darkness of innovation set upon them and whose hearts have been overcome by the result of their factionalism and whose insight has been obscured and minds corrupted by their falsifications and aversion to looking at the evidence, they are blind to its light, their

47 Qur'ān 15:9.
48 Qur'ān 11:1.
49 Qur'ān 41:3.

hearts are encased against understanding it, their ears are heavy, and they cry out that they are blind and deaf so they cannot see its radiance nor hear its call. They consider this to be complete faith in it; it is terrible that they have knowingly contented themselves with foolishness and pipe dreams.

This is the state of the vast majority of those who call themselves Muslim. They dishonour Islam by counting themselves Muslims and strengthen the case of its adversaries in their crusade against it by claiming they are the nation under its flag. They do not represent it at all, as we have demonstrated.

It is inevitable that these people will be afflicted with that which afflicted prior communities as they have followed their trajectories inch by inch and hand in hand, and they have oppressed themselves by entering into the lizard's hole which had been entered by those before them.[50] Anyone who follows the ways of a group deserves to face the same universal laws of God's ways as they did and they will not be free of the punishment God decreed for them; He had told them about the lives of those people and explained what happened to them when they transgressed and violated his laws and threw his decree behind them – He allowed them to be humiliated, made them fall into poverty, and granted their land and property to others. So, do the ones who follow their ways and walk their path expect God to do anything else with them than He did to those before them? Indeed, He has already decreed that those are His ways and that you will not find any change in His ways.[51]

These claimants of Islam will continue to face difficulties and misfortune will remain in their homes until they awaken, and they begin to awaken from their inebriation and flee to seek salvation. They wash their eyes from the impurities within and, in doing so, find this Noble Book waiting for them and preparing the means for their salvation. It helps them in this with the Holy Spirit and takes them to the fountains of knowledge so they can scoop whatever they want out of it and come to know themselves. They witness the power that was previously concealed from them, so they take one another by the hand and head towards glory without cowardice or frustration.

50 Reference to Sahih Muslim Book 34, *Ḥadīth* 6448.
51 Reference to Qur'ān 33:62.

I say to these people: Islam will never be a stumbling block to civilisation. Rather, it will reform it and refine it from its dirt. Indeed, civilisation will be among its most ardent supporters when it and its proponents come to know it. This stagnation will vanish and the strongest evidence of this is the persistence of the Book as a witness to its poor state and God's generosity in confining people to the Book who will help it and call to it and support it. Situations will help them and they will be aided by the lash of God's punishment striking those who are impervious to civilisation.

The light of this Noble Book, which has been followed by education wherever it went – East and West – must return to the forefront and it will tear down the veils of misguidance. It will return to its original home in the hearts of Muslims and will shelter itself there. Education follows it and is its close associate – it seeks its companionship and relies on it alone.

Those stagnant immobile people will say, as some opponents of the Qur'ān say: 'Time has reached its end and the last hour will soon strike. The corruption that has afflicted people, the inactivity the faith has undergone because of it, the illnesses that have afflicted it, and all the problems we can see are all signs of senility and decrepitude. There is no use in trying nor any positive result in working as the only movement is towards nothingness, and our sight should not extend beyond nothingness, and the only result we should expect for our work is nothingness.' We seek God's refuge.

These people are the offspring of ignorance and supporters of despair, and they speak nonsense. What do they know about time, such that they say it is approaching its end? The time that has passed between us and the beginning of Islam (i.e. the Hijra) is only 1,320 years, which is merely a day or part of a day in the days of God. The signs of God in the universe – despite signifying a lengthy period of time for the universe – bear witness that the time remaining for this great system cannot be calculated by anyone who attempts to do so: 'What is the matter with these people that they can barely understand what they are told?'[52]

The time between us and the beginning of Islam does not exceed the lifetimes of twenty-six generations of men if each one lived for fifty years. Can that be considered a long time in relation to a faith for all of mankind

52 Qur'ān 4:78.

such as Islam? A period of time such as this does not suffice – and it has shown that it does not suffice – to guide all people by its guidance, and if so, why is it the end of time that gets to be blamed and not their crooked ways?

God has promised that He will perfect His light and that He will make His religion prevail above all other religions. For many years He did, but then its adherents lost their way and led it to what we and they now see. The world will not come to an end until that promise is fulfilled and faith takes knowledge by the hand and they cooperate together to rectify hearts and minds. The mind will know its power and the limits of its authority and will use that which God has granted it to act as a guide while uncovering the secrets of the universe that it is able to, such that when it is covered with the majesty of God it will stop in awe and return swiftly. It will take the way of those grounded in knowledge, about whom ʿAlī ibn Abī Ṭālib said:

> They are the ones who sufficed from trying to expose the multiple veils of the unseen by their complete acknowledgement of their own ignorance in being able to explain the veiled unseen. God praised them for the acknowledgement of their inability to explain things they had no knowledge of and their avoidance of delving into matters of the universe that they were not obligated to look into was referred to as groundedness [in knowledge].

After that, think about his words:

> So limit yourself to that, and do not measure the greatness of God, Glory be to Him, according to the capacity of your mind or you will be doomed. He is the All-Powerful who, if delusion tempts one to try and assess the limit of His power, if minds try to uncover the depths of His Kingdom, if hearts attempt to unpack the mysteries of His attributes and understand the subtleties of His essence, they will swiftly be turned away in submission to Him, acknowledging that His essence is beyond their capacities to comprehend, and that the best of all minds fail to grasp His majesty even partially.

Thereby, the mind meets true intuition (i.e. the heart). In fact, intuition never separated from the mind, as long as it was sound and illuminated by the light of true faith. Do not make the mistake that some naive people have in thinking that there is a natural difference between heart and mind, as the difference between the two only occurs as a symptom of spiritual illness within the self. All discerning minds have agreed that observances by internal senses – heart or mind – are the principles of intellectual proof, such as your intuition that you exist, or your feelings of happiness, sadness, anger, pleasure, hope, etc.

We have been granted the intellect to gain insight into ends, causes, and effects, and to differentiate between the simple and the complex. As for the heart, it comprehends internal feelings, pain and pleasure, anxiety and contentment, disobedience and obedience, and other feelings that man experiences that cannot be quantified; the mind and the heart are together the eyes of the soul by which it sees, one scrutinises the internal whilst the other surveys the distance. The soul requires both and cannot benefit from one without also benefiting from the other. Sound knowledge settles the heart, and a calm heart is the best supporter of education. Complete faith is knowledge and experience, mind and heart, proof and submission, thought and intuition; if faith is predicated on one of the two then one of its supports has collapsed and it is near impossible for it to solely rely on the other. The mind and heart will not contradict each other unless a single person becomes two or a single existence becomes two.

You may ask, how is that that your mind may assume harm in doing something but you still do it by listening to your heart, and vice versa; you may perceive a benefit in something, but you still turn away from it driven by your intuition? So you say: 'This indicates a contradiction between the mind and the heart.' But I say: 'This is only a proof for one who does not know himself nor anyone else. You must look at yourself and be sure of one of two things: either that which you were convinced of is not decisive but is just something you imagined from the words of someone else, thinking it to be knowledge when it was not, or your intuition is a delusion from within you and a custom which has established itself in a position of authority in you. It is not sound intuition but a custom you inherited from those around you, which you thought were feelings emanating from your intuition, when that was not the case.'

The end of the world can only happen when knowledge and faith have joined together upon the way of the Qur'ān and people have learnt the meaning of the tradition of the Prophet, which has a correct meaning, stating: 'Contemplate the creation of God and not the essence of God.' Thereafter God will have perfected His light even if the disbelievers hate it, and they will be followed by the stagnators and the desolate. There is nothing between you and what I promise you except time in which the heedless is awakened and the ignorant is educated and the path is made clear and the crooked is straightened, and this is what is necessitated by the Divine practice in stages: 'This has been God's practice with those who went before. You will find no change in God's practices.'[53] 'The disbelievers think it is distant, but We know it to be close.'[54] 'If you help God, He will help you and make you stand firm.'[55] And He is the best helper.

Freedom of knowledge in Europe today and its relationship with the Islamic past and present

There is nothing left for us to discuss except in relation to the fourth point raised by *al-Jāmi'a*, which is:

> The possibility for science and philosophy to overcome Christian persecution in Europe, and their inability to overcome Islamic persecution, is a real sign that Christianity was more tolerant of philosophy.

It is not easy for me to believe that an erudite author like the one of *al-Jāmi'a* says these words – whilst he sees the truth with his own two eyes, knowing the language of the Westerners and having read their books on this topic, which is one of the most important historical topics. However, it is subjectivity that led him to compare Europe's current situation with Islam's current situation, dictating to his heart what his pen wrote.

Is it correct to refer to the act of surrendering to the victor as tolerance?

53 Qur'ān 33:62.
54 Qur'ān 70:6–7.
55 Qur'ān 47:7.

And to refer to helplessness, while hoping for conflict once in a position of strength, as forbearance? Or is being forcibly handcuffed against evil referred to as nobility? To the point, do you consider the cohabitation of the Pope with the King of Italy in one city and the joining of the two great thrones – the throne of the Italian kingdom and the throne of the Papacy in one capital city – to be tolerance of the Pope with the King? Is it not fairer to say it was tolerance from the King to the Pope as he was the one who held power, controlled the army, and had authority, and he could have dispossessed the Pope of those remnants that remained with him? It follows that it is proper for him to refer to the state of contentment between science and religion in Europe today as tolerance of science with religion and not tolerance of religion with science, after what took place between the two and the victory of science and its assumption of the throne of authority in all of the kingdoms and religion's contentment to follow it.

Europe's Acquisition of Civilisation from Islam and the Reasons for its General Prominence

The first reason: associations

There was a conflict between science and religion in Europe so associations and clubs were formed to support science; some chose privacy as a cover until science gained momentum, and others chose to go public. Religion used to overcome science, as explained, due to its large number of supporters and the weakness of science's supporters, until the sun of Islamic culture rose upon those lands from Spain's skies, and people's interest in this culture was followed by the radiant light of Arabian science from the East, as we have mentioned. These two lights found that people were prepared to be enlightened by them on the journey that would lead to the civilisation that they carried. This preparedness was obtained by people due to the oppression they experienced from religious leaders using their authority and their harshness in enslaving the heart and mind until human nature could no longer bear it, so human consciousness began to seek a path to liberation. So, when these two lights began to shine, these people took them as a source of guidance and faced them directly. After that, there was retribution from religion against people of learning and they were burned at the stake and exiled from their lands. Religious leaders opposed the governments and people of independent thought in the smallest of things, such as when the French kings ordered the streets of Paris to be paved according to the style which they found in Córdoba and they banned the grazing of pigs in those streets, St Antoine's clergymen were enraged and declared that the Saint's pigs must pass through the streets as they had initially been free to do so. A large riot broke out because of this which compelled the government to allow that with a decree that they must wear bells around their necks. It is said that King Philip (r. 1129–1131) died after falling from his horse when a pig was frightened by the sight of another pig with a set of bells around his neck.[1]

One could say that the clergymen at that time were able to agree to the placing of bells around the necks of pigs. So, their acceptance of that should be considered great tolerance for science or technology. It is easy for me to agree with him that such an example of tolerance with the bells on pigs did occur from time to time, but I do not think it is enough to support the civilisation that Europeans take pride in today, which we do not underestimate.

The second reason: religious pressure

Excessive need and the extremism of leaders caused the hearts of students of knowledge to burn with zeal, and their fervour never calmed. The matter grew and they discovered many facts that benefited the masses and alerted their intellects to accept whatever they were guided to. The war between them and the religious leaders had its ups and downs until the callers for religious reform were victorious – the Protestants – so the supporters of science joined them thinking that they would be fighting along with them on the path of education. One of them was the famous Erasmus, and when those seeking reform were victorious and they took control of the land, they continued executing people for thoughts that contradicted their apparent beliefs, as has been mentioned. Erasmus (d. 1536) and the supporters of free and independent thought separated themselves and left the reformers to split into varying factions fighting one another. He said: 'I did not think that reformists would also be like that: enemies of education.'[2]

These groups whose beliefs on reformation were divided waited until they were safe from their common enemy – the Roman Catholic Church.

1 'Abduh incorrectly refers to King Phillip by the epithet 'the Fat' (*al-Samīn*) whereas this was applied to his father King Louis VI (r. 1108–1137).
2 We were unable to locate a source for this quote.

Once they felt safe, they began to attack one another and the fire of war raged between them. One of the most eminent historians of them said:

> Every time one of those groups had power, they would stain their hands with crimes attempting to eradicate the others until people grew weary of that perpetual state of affairs and found, with the continual acts of retribution and the manifestation of its losses for all groups, that it is best for every group to allow one another an essential amount of freedom. Science also played its role in uncovering facts and developing literature, which was one of the strongest indicators of the losses of war and the harms to individual freedom caused by enmity to all groups. Thus, a great principle was established: the principle of tolerance and contentment to live alongside those who differed in their views. It was established from the power and oppressiveness that each group practised against the other.[3]

The third reason: revolution

There is no need for me to mention what happened during the French Revolution and what it did to faith and religious leaders, as is known. I only call the reader to consider what has already been said and what is possible for him to see in their books to know that the Christian religion in Europe did not tolerate science out of grace and nobility but was overwhelmed by its supporters who surpassed it and caused it to yield and submit. Even if it did not want to show tolerance, there was no other option.

The fourth reason: leaving Christianity

Leaders of the Christian faith were men of determination and they protected the faith; seldom could any other religious leaders match them in this. Despite their extremism in religion and their forcefulness in wielding authority over people, they used to, and still do, adopt every means to support their religion. They were the most ardent people in protecting its principal tenets and in fighting off any doubts about it, and the new

3 'Abduh here paraphrases from an unnamed historian.

knowledge only increased their means for propagating their beliefs and writings. Their zeal for spreading it and embellishing it to permeate hearts did not diminish. Nonetheless, we see that men of learning and protectors of civilisation slipped away from it and the masses were increasingly driven away from it. The French community – which used to be referred to as the daughter of the Church – became the harshest people against it and would limit the freedom of its adherents in their education and society – and the seminaries are still full of thousands of theology students and many come from countries that are distinguished by their preservation of the Christian faith across the world.

One of the Protestant leaders, during one of the speeches he gave in some French lands during the year 1901 after he had stated that Christianity, Roman or Protestant, had lost its religious essence just as it had lost its social benefit, said: 'If Christianity is nothing but Catholicism in need of reform (i.e. Roman Catholicism) or Catholicism which has already been reformed (i.e. Protestantism) then the twentieth century will have no Christianity at all.'

In the words of this orator, it is clear that he wanted to seek a new meaning for Christianity, one that aligns with the Muslim perspective on it. If he succeeds, not only will the hostility between religion and science vanish, but also between Christianity and Islam.

A return to Islam's tolerance

I will now take the reader's hand and return him to a time that has passed. I will stop with him in front of the Umayyad caliphs, the 'Abbāsid *imāms* and their viziers, the jurists, the theologians, the scholars of *Ḥadīth*, and authoritative interpreters, all around them. Surrounding them will be the men of letters, historians, doctors, astronomers, mathematicians, geographers, physicists, and other people of rational inquiry from various fields. Each of them will be working away, and when they commence their duties they approach their associate and shake his hand, the jurist with the theologian, the *Ḥadīth* scholar with the doctor, the authoritative interpreter with the mathematician, each of them seeing in their associate a helper to assist in what they are working on … let me enter with him into one of the centres of learning and we will find all of the above as equals speaking and researching together: Imām al-Bukhārī (d. 870) the great master of *Ḥadīth* taking reports from 'Imrān ibn Ḥiṭṭān the Kharijite, 'Amr ibn 'Ubayd (d. 762) the leader of the Mu'tazilites learning from al-Ḥasan al-Baṣrī (d. 728) the leader of the Sunnites among the Successors. Al-Ḥasan was asked about 'Amr and responded: 'You have asked about a man whom it is as if the angels themselves taught him and the prophets raised him. He accomplishes whatever he commits himself to. If he commanded something he would be the most resolute in following it, and if he forbade something he would be the furthest from it. I have not seen someone's exterior match their interior nor their interior match their exterior like him.'

Rather, I can lift my gaze to find Imām Abū Ḥanīfah (d. 767) in front of Imām Zayd ibn 'Alī (d. 740), founder of the Zaydi school of jurisprudence in Shiite Islam, learning the principles of law and theology from him. The only thing they find in one another is the discussion found amongst those who disagree in their efforts to to interpret law and theology in a manner that can help people whilst they are both from the same household ... I pass through those rows that differ in their approach while their purpose is the same: knowledge. Each of them believes that reasoning for an hour is better than worshipping for sixty years, as mentioned in some Prophetic reports.

The caliphs are leaders of the faith and are authoritative interpreters. Power lies in their hands and the army is under their command. Jurists, *Ḥadīth* scholars, theologians, and other authoritative interpreters are the heads of the faith and are a part of the army of the caliphs. Faith is their strength and belief is the height of their authority. The other scholars we have mentioned enjoy their encirclement by goodness, happiness, a comfortable life, and free thought, with no distinction between one who shares their faith and one who does not. Thus, the fair reader will allude to those Muslims, the supporters of that faith, and say: 'This is the true meaning of tolerance with knowledge and such a faith is characterised by nobility and forbearance. This is how faith goes hand in hand with civilisation, the art of free thought and inquiry can be learnt from these wise scholars, and in them is the spirit of reconciliation between intellect and intuition – or between the heart and the mind, as they say.'

The reader sees that there is no conflict between reason and revelation. Rather, the proponents of education and the adherents of faith had some divergence in their opinions as is the state of those who are free thinkers who have been freed from the shackles of restraint and cured from the illness of conformity. There was no censuring nor name-calling between them as none of them said about the other: 'He is a heretic or an unbeliever or a blameworthy innovator or the like.' None of them would be harmed unless they threatened the social system or violated the safety of the masses; in that case, they would be like a leprous limb that is cut off to avoid harm to the entire body.

Knowledge's dependence on religion and the contagion of bigotry amongst Muslims

When have Muslims been enthusiastic about excommunication and accusing one another of immorality, labelling X as a blameworthy innovator and Y as a heretic?

We have already alluded to this sickness and now we say that it began with them once insecurity seeped into their faith and tribulations consumed their people of insight – those tribulations that were caused by enemies of the faith in the East and the West who aimed to reduce its authority and weaken its foundations – and those whose souls had not been combined with the spirit of the faith. Furthermore, Muslims began to introduce innovations under the guise of revering the rites of Islam, in accordance with those among them from Christian nations and others. They were raised forgetting the history of their religion and the wisdom of the earliest generations about it and they would be content with the views of the one they saw as a leader – the faux scholar. The ignorant Muslims took over their affairs and the misled ones tried to guide them. In the midst of that, religious extremism occurred and the fires of animosity blazed amongst its people of reflection. It became easy for all of them, due to their ignorance of the faith, to accuse one another of disbelief for the slightest reason. Every time their ignorance of the faith increased so did their wrongful extremism, thus knowledge, thought, and inquiry – inseparable attributes of the Islamic faith – were all considered detested things. That which used to be a necessary requirement of the faith for them became forbidden by it.

I do not deem the reader to be incorrect if he claims that the Muslim has gained the name *zandaqah* (heresy) from his neighbours, as they used to use the conjugations of the word 'heresy'. Or if he claims that expedient excommunication has spread amongst Muslims like a contagion from adherents of zealous groups. Indeed, it is a weakness of religious temperament among Muslims that has facilitated the incredibly quick spread of the contagion due to their ignorance of the faith's principles and core features. Whenever temperament weakens it paves the way for disease, as is known.

When Muslims were real scholars of their faith, they were equally scholars of worldly sciences and leaders of the world. When they were afflicted by the disease of ignorance of their faith, they were routed from existence and became prey for the hunter and food for the forager. Did the ignorance of Muslims stop at excommunicating those who differed with them in matters of faith or those who took the approach of the philosophers or something close to that? No. Rather, their ignorance reached those who were leaders of the faith and servers of the Qur'ān and prophetic paradigm. The books of Imām al-Ghazālī (d. 1111) were taken to Granada and, after the Muslims had been guided by them for an extended period of time, the people of that city were stirred up by ignorance, and the tongues of the faux scholars from the Amazighs accused the Muslims of immorality and causing misguidance, so all those books were gathered, particularly *The Revival of the Religious Sciences* and they were put in the public street and burned.[4] People who consider themselves Muslim say about Ibn Taymiyya (d. 1328) – and he was the most knowledgeable person about the *Sunna* and the most ardent in protecting the faith – that he was misguided and misled others.[5] Following the footsteps of these people are blind conformers who fill their mouths with such vilifications. They carry their sins and the sins of those who follow them until Judgement Day.

4 Abū Ḥāmid al-Ghazālī was one of the most prominent and influential theologians of Sunni Islam; Amazigh is the contemporary self-name for the Berber peoples, a diverse grouping of distinct ethnic groups indigenous to North Africa who predate the arrival of the Arabs to the region; the event ʿAbduh refers to here took place during the period of the Almoravid dynasty (1054–1147).

5 Ibn Taymiyya was a prominent Islamic scholar who influenced a number of reform movements that sought to reformulate traditional ideologies by a return to the original sources.

Neglect of the statements of the earliest Muslims and the state of the religious sciences and their students

Muslims have neglected the sciences of their religion and the statements of their earliest predecessors such that you cannot find in their hands today one of the books of Abū al-Ḥasan al-Ash'arī (d. 936) or Abū Manṣūr al-Māturīdī (d. 944).[6] Moreover, you can barely see one of the works of Abū Bakr al-Bāqillānī (d. 1013) or Abū Isḥāq al-Isfarāyīnī (d. 1027).[7] If you searched for a book of one of these *Imāms* in the libraries of Muslims, the search would fatigue you and you would hardly find a reliable copy of one of those books.

There were many books of Qur'ānic exegesis written in the third Islamic century up until the sixth. Some examples are the books of exegesis by al-Ṭabarī (d. 932), Abū Muslim al-Iṣfahānī (d. 934), al-Qurṭubī (d. 1273), al-Jaṣṣās (d. 981), al-Ghazālī, Ibn al-'Arabī (d. 1240), and many others.[8] Those books contain the opinions of those *Imāms* and their methods of interpreting the Sharī'a and its wisdoms which no student of the religion can do without. Would the industrious researcher find a reliably verified copy of these great books, other than by chance? Is it befitting for a community that claims it is faithful and that it has venerable forefathers to disassociate itself from the traces of those forefathers and to leave their writings as worm food and a cushion for the dirt? Did anything like this ever happen with those who studied Christian theology in the past?

The state of those who study the Islamic sciences has become something

6 Abū al-Ḥasan al-Ash'arī was an Islamic theologian who played a key role in the development of Sunni theology, particularly known for his synthesis of rationalism and traditionalism in the Ash'arite School; Abū Manṣūr al-Māturīdī was an Islamic theologian who founded the Māturīdī School, emphasising a rationalist approach within Sunni Islam and contributing to the development of Islamic theology.

7 Abū Bakr al-Bāqillānī was an Islamic theologian, central to the Ash'arite School, known for his influential works in reconciling reason and revelation, shaping Sunni theology and addressing theological challenges within the Islamic tradition; Abū Isḥāq al-Isfarāyīnī played a prominent role in representing the Ash'arite school of theology in Nishapur during the late tenth and early eleventh centuries.

8 Muḥammad ibn Jarīr al-Ṭabarī was an Islamic scholar and historian whose comprehensive works significantly contributed to Islamic exegesis and historiography; al-Iṣfahānī was an Arabic prose stylist and literary figure; Abū 'Abdullāh al-Qurṭubī was an Islamic scholar and jurist best known for his influential exegesis of the Qur'ān titled *Al-Jāmi' li-Aḥkām al-Qur'ān*; Shams al-Dīn al-Jaṣṣās was an Islamic jurist and scholar known for his contributions to Islamic legal theory, particularly in the Ḥanafī School; Muḥyi al-Dīn Ibn al-'Arabī was an Islamic mystic and philosopher and is celebrated as a key figure Sufism.

that is to be elegised in most Muslim lands as they only read the abridgements written by later generations. The most intelligent among them only learns what the expressions in those treatises allude to but he is unable to learn how to investigate their proofs, verify their propositions, and distinguish between their advantages and drawbacks. He receives them as he receives the Book of God or the sayings of the Prophet – peace and blessings of God be upon him – accepting them without question. If someone challenges him on some of its points, he is unable to verify them and the discussion ends with him saying: 'This is what they said.' Such would be their reaction even if an opinion is not agreed upon, or even if it was not said by anyone other than the author who wrote that work, and perhaps the author was a person whom one of the *Salaf*, if he saw him, would not be pleased to have a student who learns what he teaches.

In Syria, the Hijaz, Tunis, and Algeria, the study of religious sciences has almost ended, and it has declined considerably in Morocco, with the exception of only some regions of the Sahara which maintain an interest in it. That is either due to difficult teaching methods and the long time-commitment required – and people's needs prevent them from spending their lives doing something that does not provide for their needs – or due to parents preferring to raise their children according to modern curricula from Europe, or in other schools which are completely secular – and if they contain any traces of religious studies, they are subpar. Or it is because of the laxity and decline that results from blind conformity and stagnation. Consequently, you find Muslims have been overcome by ignorance of their faith and heresies have taken hold of them in all spheres, and any true connection between them and their early predecessors has been severed, such that if the vast majority were presented with something that the early predecessors agreed upon, they would rebuke it, deem it odd, and consider it an innovation in the religion. It is true what Omar Khayyam (d. 1131) said about them in one of his Persian poems addressing the Prophet: 'Those who came after you embellished, adorned, and ornamented your religion for you such that if you saw it, you would not recognise it.'[9]

9 Omar Khayyam was a Persian polymath best known for his *Rubaiyat*, a collection of quatrains that blend poetry, philosophy, and reflections on life. We were unable to locate the source for this quote.

This group of Muslims – which is the majority today – have denied their true religion and have acted hostilely towards it. They are resentful towards its adherents who sincerely serve it and have chosen as their role models some individual scholars who were not particularly trustworthy according to the earlier generations, nor does the religion permit them to be imitated. When real scholars and scholarship are harmed by such people, are they then to blame them or the religion of Islam itself, the religion of Muhammad, the religion of the Qur'ān, the religion of attested prophetic practice, the religion of the rightly guided caliphs and those who followed them from the earliest generations?

Knowledge's affiliation with Islam and its disassociation from all else

I say the truth – and reality supports me – that they (i.e. Muslims) did not act hostilely towards learning nor did it act hostilely towards them until the day they diverged from their faith and stopped earnestly studying. Anytime they were distanced from knowledge of the religion, they were distanced from knowledge of the material world and, as a result, were prohibited from the fruits of exercising the intellect. Anytime they engaged extensively with the religious sciences they equally engaged with natural sciences and triumphed over time. As for others, anytime they connected to religion and strove to preserve it, knowledge refused to have anything to do with them, and scowled at them with its gloomy face turned towards them, and anytime they distanced themselves from religion, it made peace with them and smiled at them. Accordingly, they state that knowledge is the domain of the mind and that it is not right for religion to have any interaction with the mind nor to leave any impression upon it. They say religion relates to the sentiments of the heart and there is no connection between what the heart finds and what the mind acquires. Thus, the separation between the mind and religion is decisive, and there is no way to join the two – may God show tolerance with them for what they have deemed to be tolerance with knowledge, claiming that knowledge is religion's enemy and that it is impossible for there to be any peace between them.

Do you know the reason for Muslims' persecution of knowledge? I say 'persecution,' but I do not mean that which occurred with Christian communities such as the intense effort to eradicate its proponents, invent new kinds of punishments for them, and innovate new torture apparatuses, condemning their suspects to the death penalty for nothing more than an accusation. None of this took place with the Muslims, not in their days of knowledge production nor in their times of ignorance. Rather, I simply mean by 'persecution' the disinclination towards knowledge, mocking its proponents with degrading nicknames, hurling insults at them, and isolating them.

There is no doubt that you are now certain of the reason for what this author referred to as 'persecution'. It is because of their ignorance of their faith. The only medication that can cure them of this sickness is their return to having knowledge of their faith and pondering it so as to arrive at its secrets and reach the reality of what it calls for. Religion was the mutual friend between them and knowledge, and once it departed, people became ignorant and intimacy was replaced by estrangement.

The callers to Islam

Are there any more true callers to knowledge among the Muslims or knowledgeable callers to the essence of the faith who were opposed by the laity? Has the number of those callers increased in Muslim lands the way it increased in Europe from the mid-fourteenth century until the early seventeenth century and what followed? No. Instead, what we see are individual people of truth who have separately appeared at various times, with there being perhaps only four of them, or more, in a single century. Once they begin working in their fields, they make a handful of statements and good-natured people start to take notice, until politics (we seek God's refuge from it) starts to observe what could come out of it. So, they quickly suppress their breaths before they can plant thoughts in a single heart; the light is extinguished and darkness spreads.

Did the author consider these political acts as suppression of knowledge in order to protect the faith? Every erudite author is far above this way of thinking! Rather, they are blows against the faith that do not differ from the blows given by the likes of our author. So, they cannot be considered proofs against the faith in the view of any fair person.

The imitator is always below the imitated

One may say that Muslims inherited stagnation, blind imitation, the abandonment of education, belief in a conflict between this world and the next and between reason and revelation, and other erroneous things that they believe in from previous communities, especially the religious groups closest to them. Then why did they not also imitate the Christians in evangelising, expanding their knowledge, and acknowledging whatever they took from them? Why have they not divided themselves into two groups as the Christians did: one which is purely devoted to the hereafter in their monasteries and hermitages, and the other which works in this world to support themselves and those of the first group, thereby protecting themselves and the others from their enemies? Why do you see the Muslims as having weakened and lost their nerve, tired of the sciences of their own faith as I have recounted, thereby becoming the people furthest away from knowing the means of acquiring wealth and attaining power and honour? They have thrown themselves into the current of predestination – as they say – not knowing where it will take them. Then, you see them as the most desirous for life, hankering after any cheap gain, and most of them are neither successful in religious terms nor in worldly terms, so why the paradox?

I respond that you have forgotten that the imitator is always below the one being imitated. The imitator simply looks at the external acts of the one being imitated and is not aware of its inner component or what it is based on, so he acts without a system and has no guiding principle. As a result, the Muslims have descended into a worse state than the ones they imitate, especially as they have mixed their imitations and have added things that have nothing to do with their faith. They have become like the wanderer who is pulled in many directions; he follows all of them at once and thus his journey fails and ends in extreme exhaustion until he drops to the ground, rests, and rises again to act upon guidance, or perish.

When Muslims were people of scholarship, they had two eyes: one which looked to the material world and the other to the hereafter. When they began imitating, one of the eyes closed and a foreign speck flew into the other so they lost track of both goals, and they will never see through them both until they open the eye that closed and clean the other one.

Reform and reformers

One could ask: How can you claim that there are few callers to education and faith among Muslims though we hear their voices multiplied in Egypt, Syria, and other places these days? Everyone is saying: 'My religion and my faith,' 'Islam and Muslims,' 'Qur'ān and *Sunna*,' 'Islam's former glory,' 'its righteous predecessors,' 'learn,' 'educate,' 'old books,' 'new books,' etc. It would seem that there are many callers to education and people alerting others to return to the principles of the Islamic faith. Yet, what we see from most Muslims are deaf ears and blind eyes preventing what these people are calling for.

I can respond that there are not many honest ones among them as the majority of them rarely have pure intentions. You will find that most of them exploit these words to earn some pennies. This is apparent as they articulate these words but hardly study their meanings at all in order to arrive at their reality. Rather, they are empty words that they use like froth which quickly disintegrates. As for the honest ones, despite how few they are, people have begun listening to what they say and seeking guidance based on their knowledge, specifically in matters of faith and combining it with the good of the temporal world, especially in India and among the Muslims of Russia. But reform is not a breeze that is set in motion and cleans the Earth from East to West in a short period of time, so keep waiting.

One may ask further: 'Why are there not more of such people as there were with the Europeans in the past, such that they overcame the oppressive politicians and won the favour of the fair-minded ones, who can awaken the Muslims from their prolonged slumber? And why are the people of insight among them still so few in number and disunited, speaking softly rather than raising their voices, and there are no active callers to education among them? Is this not a proof against Islam and a reason to blame it?'

I respond: 'Muslims' luck cannot be greater than those they are imitating. Rather, it is expected that it will be worse. It took more than 1,000 years for education to become prevalent in Christendom, for the notion of individual freedom to emerge and for the scientific movement to pervade it to an extent that reformed human society after many incitements, and conflict after conflict. With Muslims, it is only 800 years that have passed since heresies became deep-rooted among them and darkened their lives.

Thus, they entered the lizard's hole which had been entered by those before them. With this in mind, the same amount of time has not yet passed for Muslims, and they will hopefully reach their goal by its end. I hope the same period of time will not pass before Muslims reach the end they deserve and attain the best in both: sacred and worldly.'

The difference between the two types of fanaticism

Nonetheless, it is not in accordance with the law of justice for Muslims to be mentioned alongside the majority of Christians on the matter of religious fanaticism, let alone to say that Muslims were even more excessive in this matter. The evidence shows us that Muslim fanaticism took the form of words, whereas the fanaticism of the Christians took form in their actions and treatment of one another. One who is seeking the truth need only let his thoughts go, for example, to the Dutch colonies in the East and in Transvaal before its fall and the Natalia Republic in the South, then let it return to some of the Russian provinces in the North twenty years ago, then to Algeria and the regions to the West of it, in order to understand their severity in dealing with non-Christians. Their fanaticism towards their people reached a level that humanity would look at distrustfully, and modernity makes no excuse for that.

A researcher only needs to look at the words written by French authors to know that they were in a state of confusion regarding their situation with the Muslims, wanting their government to maintain equanimity with their possessions of Muslim lands, but they could not find a way to achieve that due to their principle in dealing with them, which was harshness and excessive cruelty towards Muslims in particular. Men of letters searched for a way to attain that equanimity while maintaining that harshness, but God prevented them from finding what they were looking for as they sought to combine two opposites in one place, which is an impossibility as explained by their own philosophers.

Hanotaux's recent opinion

Monsieur Hanotaux has for years written on his search for a way to govern Muslims and on the principle by which they should be dealt with in the lands that are controlled by the French. Readers continue to remember what he wrote in the chapters of his article after he studied the subject for three years and saw how his view was not well received by Muslims. Now he returned to the same subject but with a different opinion. I will summarise what the newspapers transmitted from his speech given to the Geographical Society in March of this year relating to Africa, restricting myself to that which relates to our discussion here.[10]

He stated in his speech: 'The principles which must be acted upon in Africa are in opposition to the old principles which colonial politics ran on in the past.' He then explained these new principles, which the governed should be ruled by: 'They are peace and justice.' Then he said: 'We owe them peace and justice just as we owe them religious tolerance. I am only gently alluding to this dangerous issue which connects to everything that incites human emotions, so I say that European civilisation has found along its journey in Africa, especially in the North, that magnificent ancient religion – the religion of Islam – which is the most widespread in that region (i.e. North Africa). This religion propagates belief in One God and makes monotheistic faith the source of all individual and social virtues. That faith intensely occupies a believer such that he cannot turn away from it. Thus, it is necessary for us to be tolerant in this matter. Rather, tolerance alone is not enough but we must study this religion and put forth our best effort to understand it. We must adopt the Islamic saying that "There is no compulsion in religion" as a rule that we must abide by and respect the Islamic faith and protect it from any unforeseen difficulty. There is no problem with quoting the words of ʿAbd al-Qādir al-Jazāʾirī (d. 1883) on this: "Adherents of the three faiths are like three brothers born of three different mothers."'[11]

Before commenting on the above, I ask the reader if he has ever heard any such words from one who is equal to al-Jazāʾirī in terms of his genealogical relation to the Prophet or in his standing with members of his

10 The year was 1902.

11 ʿAbduh here notes that he is summarising Hanotaux's speech, but no reference is provided for the original speech's publication in print; Al-Jazāʾirī was an Algerian religious and military leader who led the resistance against French colonisation in the nineteenth century. Renowned for his commitment to Islamic values, he became a symbol of anti-colonial resistance, establishing an Islamic state in Algeria and leaving a lasting impact on its history.

religious community or his sound understanding of creed? Or has he heard anything close to it from one who was not his equal from other faiths?

You see Hanotaux advising his people to adopt a new method of governing Muslims which was peace, justice, and tolerance for Muslims to remain Muslims, to respect their rights and to allow them to practise their religion. This was considered a new principle, the likes of which had not been tried before. Will the French government respond to his request? We will see. Thus, is it appropriate for a fair-minded person to bring up peace when fanaticism is mentioned, while there remains this level of fanaticism in existence?

Policy of the English regarding tolerance

Yes, we do not deny that among the European nations there is one who knows how to govern those who do not share their faith and how to respect their beliefs and customs. It is the English nation. It is the only Christian nation that is capable of real tolerance, and it is not difficult for us to say that the origin of that was her commanders and army generals in the Crusades who had the strongest ties with the Muslim ruler and commanders. The English stood out in that dark time by studying the beliefs and customs of the Muslims and they conveyed much of that back to their lands; the veil of fanaticism never obscured the light of truth from their eyes. The effects of that became clear in a number of their writers such as Walter Scott (d. 1832), Schiller (d. 1805), and others, well before the pens of non-English writers appeared by a number of years.[12] Thus, we may say without fear of reproach that this noble quality – the quality of allowing freedom for religious adherents to fulfil their obligations while respecting what they respect – is one of the greatest qualities that non-Muslims inherited from Muslims. Is there anyone who would disagree with me that an Islam that was safe from heresies was a teacher to the English and, from it, they adopted this quality? Do you not see that their method is close to the method of the Muslims in the days when they really used to be Muslims?

12 Although ʿAbduh is discussing the English in this section, neither of the examples he gives here are English. Walter Scott was Scottish and Johann Christoph Friedrich von Schiller was German.

They were content with people obeying the laws and paying their taxes then they maintained the system of justice between them, as much as politics allowed, and did not differentiate between one religion and another. Such was the state of the Muslims, and that was based upon a principle that was fairer and kinder.

Conclusion

If one were to ask: 'Does this essay not have an end? Does extended discussion not engender boredom and sluggishness?' I say that I direct these words of mine to those who insatiably seek understanding and who are avid for knowledge, and I think such people will seek something even more comprehensive than this essay and far longer, as the subject matter is significant and words about it, no matter how plentiful, fall short. As for the weary reader, he is weak-minded and his will is not firm, his thoughts are shackled and he has little ambition in matters both long and short. They are not addressed, nor are they of any value. Despite that, I will end here and I will wait for another opportunity to provide a detailed explanation of the issue of Islam's sicknesses, the effects of heresies, and the issues that have afflicted Muslims as a result.

Before I leave the reader, I want him to note that, in what I summarise in these chapters, there was no intent to criticise an individual or a group, as the reader will know from the form and content of the essays, which are free from polemics, and the avoidance of any words which carry the scent of criticising another. He will know from this avoidance that this is a view that we prepared to nourish ourselves with, and that we used it to support those we are responsible for in our community, and it did not occur to us when we found ourselves preparing it to withhold it from others. Rather, if a night traveller was guided to the light of our fire and requested hospitality from us, we would share with them what is livelier than the spirit of life itself and what is more pleasurable than the ethic of forbearance, if God wills.

Bibliography

Abdel Haleem, M.A.S. 2008. *The Qur'an: A New Translation*. Oxford: Oxford World's Classics.

Abdelnour, Gamal M. 2019. Review of 'Reforming Modernity', *Journal of Islamic Ethics,* Vol. 3, Nos. 1–2, Dec. Leiden and Boston: Brill: 238–43.

__________________. 2021. *A Comparative History of Catholic and Aš'arī Theologies of Truth and Salvation: Inclusive Minorities, Exclusive Majorities*. Leiden and Boston: Brill.

__________________. 2022. *The Higher Objectives of Islamic Theology: Toward a Theory of Maqāṣid al-ʿAqīda*. Oxford and New York: Oxford University Press.

ʿAbduh, Muḥammad. 1988. *al-Islām wa-l Naṣrāniyya maʿa al-ʿIlm wa-l-Madaniyya*, 2nd edn. Beirut: Dār al-Hadātha.

__________________. 1996. *Risālat al-tawḥīd*, Trans. Ishāq Musaʿad and Kenneth Cragg. London: George Allen & Unwin Ltd.

__________________ and Riḍā, Rashīd. 1367 H/1947. *Tafsīr al-manār*, 2nd edn. Cairo: Maṭbaʿat al-Manār.

Adamec, Ludwig W. 2017. *Historical Dictionary of Islam,* 3rd edn. London and New York: Rowman.

Adams, Charles, C. 1968. *Islam and Modernism in Egypt: A Study of the Modern Reform Movement Inaugurated by Muḥammad ʿAbduh*, 2nd edn. New York: Russell.

Ahmed, Shahab. 2016. *What Is Islam? The Importance of Being Islamic*. Princeton, NJ, and Oxford: Princeton University Press.

Akhavi, Shahrough. 2013. 'Sayyid Qutb', in *The Oxford Handbook of*

Islam and Politics, ed. John L. Esposito, and Emad El-Din Shahin. Oxford: Oxford University Press.

Amīn, ʿUthmān. [n.d.] *Muḥammad ʿAbduh: rāʾid al-fikr al-miṣrī.* Cairo: al-Majlis al-ʿAlā liʾl-Thaqāfa.

Anṭūn, Faraḥ. 2007. *Ibn Rushd wa Falsafatuhu*, ed. Ṭayyib Al-Tīzīnī, 2nd edn. Bayrūt: Dār al-Farābī.

Ayyub, Mahmoud. 1974. 'Islam and Christianity: A Study of Muhammad Abduh's View of the Two Religions', *Humaniora Islamica*, Vol. 2: 121–37.

Buğday, Korkut. 2009. *The Routledge Introduction to Literary Ottoman*, trans. Jerold C. Frakes. Abingdon: Routledge.

Draper, John W. 1877. *History of the Conflict between Religion and Science*, 10th edn. London: Henry S. King & Co.

Frame, John M. 1994. *Apologetics to the Glory of God.* Phillipsburg: Presbyterian & Reformed.

Fuyumi, Katsuhata. 2009. 'Muhammad ʿAbduh and John William Draper', *Annals of Japan Association for Middle East Studies*, Vol. 25, No. 1: 165–85. https://doi.org/10.24498/ajames.25.1_165.

Gibbon, Edward. 1776 (1823). *The History of the Decline and Fall of the Roman Empire*, Vol. VI, Chapter LII. Reprint. London: W Baynes & Son.

Guizot, François. 2013. *History of Civilization in Europe*, Trans. William Hazlitt. Carmel: Liberty Fund Inc.

Hamdeh, Emad, 'Shaykh Google as Ḥāfiẓ al-ʿAṣr The Internet, Traditional "ʿUlamā," and Self Learning', *The American Journal of Islam and Society*, Vol. 37, No. 1–2 (2020): 67–102.

Hanotaux, Gabriel. 1317H/1990. 'Al-Islām. 2.' *al-Muʾayyad* Vol. 11, No. 3036: 1–2.

Hourani, Albert. 1962. *Arabic Thought in the Liberal Age 1798–1939.* London: Oxford University Press.

Ibn Khaldūn, ʿAbd al-Raḥmān. 2004. *Muqaddima*, 1st ed., ed. Abdullāh M. Darwīsh. Damascus: Maktabat al-Hidāya.

Ibn Mājah, Abū ʿAbd Allāh. [n.d.]. *Sunan*, ed. Muḥammad Nāṣir al-Dīn al- Albānī. Riyadh: Dār al-Maʿārif.

ʿImāra, Muḥammad. 1993. *Al-Aʿmāl al-kāmila liʾl-imām Muḥammad ʿAbduh*, 1st edn. Cairo and Beirut: Dār al-Shurūq.

Kateman, Ammeke. 2019. *Muḥammad ʿAbduh and His Interlocutors: Conceptualizing Religion in a Globalizing World*. Leiden and Boston: Brill.

King James Bible. 2008 (Original work published 1769). Oxford: Oxford University Press.

Leaman, Oliver (2015). *The Biographical Encyclopedia of Islamic Philosophy.* London: Bloomsbury.

Le Bon, Gustave. 1884 (1980). *La civilisation des Arabes*. Reprint. Paris: Le Sycomore.

López, Fernando B. 2014. 'The Genocidal Islamophobia of a Late Nineteenth-Century French Anti-Semite: D. Kimon and The Pathology of Islam,' *Islam and Christian–Muslim Relations*, Vol. 25, No. 1: 101–16.

Mestyan, Adam. 2020. 'Khedive', *Encyclopaedia of Islam*, 3rd edn, Vol. 2. Leiden and Boston: Brill.

Nasr, Vali R. 2006. *The Sunni Revival: How Conflicts within Islam Will Shape the Future*. New York: Norton.

Riḍā, Rashīd. 2006. *Tārīkh al-imām Muḥammad ʿAbduh*, 2nd edn, Vol. 1. Cairo: Dār al-Faḍīla.

Rouayheb, Khaled el. 2015. *Islamic Intellectual History in the Seventeenth Century: Scholarly Currents in the Ottoman Empire and the Maghreb*. New York: Cambridge University Press.

al-Samʿāni, ʿAbd al-Karīm. [n.d.] *al-Ansāb*, Vol. 3 (Hyderabad: al-ʿUthmāniyya).

al-Sanūsī, Yūsuf. 1835. *Risāla fī ʿilm al-tawḥīd: Umm al-barahīn*. Cairo: Bulaq.

Scharbrodt, Oliver. 2022. *Muhammad ʿAbduh: Modern Islam and the Culture of Ambiguity*. London: I.B. Tauris.

Sedgwick, Mark. 2010. *Muhammad Abduh: Makers of the Islamic World*. Oxford: Oneworld.

Taylor, Isaac. 1888. 'Christian Lectures on Buddhism, and Plain Facts about the Same, by Buddhists', *Lucifer* Vol. 2, No. 8: 142–9.

Witzel, Michael. 'Autochthonous Aryans? The Evidence from Old Indian and Iranian Texts,' *Electronic Journal of Vedic Studies* Vol. 7, No. 3 (2001): 1–93, http://dx.doi.org/10.11588/ejvs.2001.3.830.

Online source

Papal Encyclicals Online. *Decrees of the First Vatican Council: Council Fathers 1868*. https://www.papalencyclicals.net/councils/ecum20.htm (accessed on 3 February 2024)

Index